OUR MONEY STORIES

A SIX-WEEK NO B.S. HOLISTIC GUIDE TO FINANCIAL WELLNESS

By

Eugenie´George MBA, CFEI

THIS BOOK IS DEDICATED TO

For Breonna Taylor and the 40 Women of Color that shared me their stories

Also, my family: Without y'all, I wouldn't have a story!

You are the wind beneath my wings. Without these folks, I wouldn't have been able to write this book so for this, I say thank you!

Pebbles Armwood

Janet Cruz Bisonó

Mehrsa Baradaran

Black CFPs

Joy Harden Bradford

Douglas and Heather Boneparth

Erica Booth

Candance Box

Rose Brewer

Jolie Dawn

Danielle Desir

Joy DeGruy

Tiffany Grant

Rianka Dorsainvil

FPA Activate

Timothy Ferriss

Food Heaven Podcast

Marie Forleo

Ashley Fox

Dr. Nadine Harriss

Minda Harts

Lewis Howes

Joe Holberg

Marcus Anthony Hunter

Anodea Judith

Michael Kitces

Phoung Loung

Nikyla Mariah

Antoinette Minor

Angela Moore

Carl Richards

Kristy Runzer

Barbara Robles

On the Goga

Amanda Steinberg

Farnosh Torabi

That's So Retrograde Ladies

Bari Tessler

Kristin Wong

WOC Podcascasters

Betsy Leondar-Wright

Muhammad Yunnus

DISCLAIMER

I have tried to recreate events, locales, and conversations from my memories of them. In order to maintain their anonymity in some instances, I have changed the names of individuals and places, I may have changed some identifying characteristics and details such as physical properties, occupations and places of residence. This book is not intended as a substitute for the medical advice of physicians.

BONUS

Would you like a printed out copy of your Six Week Financial Wellness Plan?

Included is all 6 Week Exercises

Log on to

https://eugeniegeorge.com/financialwellnessplan

Passcode: Ancestral

Contents

Introduction

If you don't hate me at some point throughout this book, then I have not done my job correctly. This book is intentionally going to open a can of kick-butt when it comes to money. Money is very uncomfortable, and it can bring up a lot of pleasure and pain. Our money has so much to do with our daily conversations.

You live in a world where you can find the answers to life's most in-depth questions with the click of a button. Or you can look at trillions of pictures of cats on your computer screen. You live in a time where you can have a co-worker that works in Lagos, Nigeria, working on the same company goals as you. But you also live in a time where countries are separating themselves from the global conversation. Governments are ignoring significant issues such as global warming or the need for educating people in developing countries. With all these problems, it makes you want to look at cats on your phone as a way to cope. I want you to have the opportunity to look at your B.S. and laugh and cry about it. I want you to create a plan where you can make weekly check-ins with yourself and see if you are financially well.

As a Certified Financial Educator, I've had the privilege of talking to all walks of life with their experiences with money. Through these conversations, it occurred to me that most people who are working their money stories and their future get bombarded with overworking or are helping others figure out their life, ignoring their own. Through interviews and teaching money classes in corporations and nonprofits, it is clear that we all have blind spots in our money habits. But the key is to create a holistic version of our money. By looking at our past, establishing awareness with our ancestry, and building a new money story, we will be able to break barriers in our lives. The layout of the book is in four phases:

Phase 1: Our Money Stories

Phase 2: Financial Wellness 101

Phase 3: Writing Your Financial Wellness Plan

Phase 4: Finding your Financial BFF

Phase One: Our Money Stories

Money stories are the conversations and habits that you have with your money. They may be conscious or unconscious, but they are your beliefs about money and how you use it.[i] In this portion of the book, you will learn more about my money story. I've never shared my trauma because I had to unlearn a lot of money ideas. Learning about my story will help you understand how layered a money story can be.

Together we'll put on our thinking caps, learn about the money narratives around Women of Color. For the brevity of this book, I chose to highlight Women of Color in the United States. The cultures that I decided to research are African American, Asian American, Latinx American, and Native American Women. I interviewed 40 women, and I asked them what their money story was like growing up. I then researched all of the policies that have been in place to discriminate against Women of

Color and their money stories. There were a lot of themes that were unique and similar to each experience, but I knew that I wanted to provide a unique narrative for Women of Color.

Phase Two: Financial Wellness 101

Financial Wellness is the latest buzzword in personal finance. The term financial wellness means to be financially stable. Because it is a buzzword, there isn't a good definition to explain how you can achieve it. It becomes a woo-woo blanket statement, but it doesn't have to be. In this portion of the book, we'll take a bird's eye view of the term. We'll use the eight pillars of wellness to see how each component fits in with your money story.

Phase Three: Writing Your Financial Wellness Plan

This portion of the book is where practice meets theory. We organize your money life. It is your new plan to figure out what to do with your money. In each part, I guide you and help you figure out what your patterns and habits are with spending. All of these techniques will help you throughout your life. Your financial wellness plan would be a reusable step-by-step process if you chose it to be. The more I teach these concepts to people, the more I recognize that building money habits and systems can take years to process. In all honesty, it took me three years to get some practices in place without feeling any shame.

Phase Four: Finding your Financial BFFs

A Financial BFF is an accountability group, friend, or financial professional that will help you with your money story without shame or guilt. Your BFFs won't sugarcoat your money woes; they help you uncover blind spots. Some BFFs come and go, but some become lifelong partners. It's all a process.

In this last portion, we're talking about the ins and outs of financial BFFs. There were countless times where I would have interactions with people after financial wellness training, and they would ask me what they needed to do next. I would scramble around to find the right people to help them, but I didn't have a list of people. I would have to explain to people the difference between a financial coach and a CFP, but all of those terms deserve clear definitions. I realized that different people require different financial BFFs in their lives, so I created a detailed BFF guide to help you figure out what friend you need.

Part One

OUR MONEY STORIES

Chapter 1
Getting Evicted

I can remember when I first saw the pink eviction notice on my apartment door. I was coming home from pitching a business idea to a potential client, only to find my door had been bolted and locked. As I picked up the pink slip, I could feel the sharp pain in my heart. I failed, and the pink slip of rejection was a wake-up call that I had. But I wasn't always this way. How got to rock bottom became a fast transition from oh yeah to damn it.

For years, I worked for companies and was an avid saver. I was an elementary school teacher, and then I moved on to work for Educational Technology companies. Before starting a business, I managed to keep my rent low, and I always had at least ten thousand dollars in the bank. When I transitioned to a small business owner, I lost all my hard-working money. I began to overwork, taking any job that I could. I was working for Free99 for many projects or clients. Working 80 hours a week, I lost track of how I was spending and how I was underearning

Within a short year of draining my savings, I started spending more money on self- help and money classes, which cost more than I was used to. I thought if I could *feel* the abundance, then I could make it. They were telling me to spend over my limit. All of the mindset stuff was great, but there was no real practical advice on how to manage my money. I had self-help fatigue and was left with unanswered questions.

During this WTF version of my life, I reconnected with an old friend from middle school; we'll call her Michelle. Michelle was a successful business owner in California. It was nice to reconnect with her because, unlike me, Michelle was a rebel. Even when we were kids, I can remember Michelle telling our 6th grade Social Studies teacher just what she thought about the Mesopotamia period. "The Mesopotamians wouldn't help wounded people or save orphans in Mexico," she would say. Michelle was a realist, even at 12 years old. It was something that I admired about her; she was a rebel but cared.

Michelle started a successful travel business through thrifting, hustling, and being adventurous. Many of her business ventures required her to rub elbows with the likes of Richard Branson and Tony Hseih, CEO of Zappos. In addition to jet-setting the world, she set up funds for the Peruvian Hearts Foundation, WildCoast, Sports for Exceptional Athletes of San Diego, Urban Angels Volunteer group, and others. We would chat and laugh about working too much and not making that much money. Yes, Michelle was a badass entrepreneur, but she didn't vibe with saving money. I found this to be interesting. How could someone make so much money but not save any of it?

One September, Michelle texted me that she was headed to Philadelphia to see her brother and wanted to meet up with me. I was so excited to see my friend in the flesh. We had chatted virtually for so long; I couldn't wait to party with her on the East Coast. We agreed that I'd see her in November.

November passed. I texted and asked her when she was traveling to the East Coast. She said that she broke up with her boyfriend. And she would get back to me. I texted her at the end of December to the check-in...No response. For me, that was okay because I was working 80 hours a week. I did not pay attention too much because I was hustling. December 31st rolls around, and I see an Instagram post of Michelle drinking a *Corona* and doing yoga on a beach. In perfect influencer fashion, she posted that this was going to be the best year ever! I thought nothing of it and was happy to see her life was back in order.

Three days later, a friend found Michelle dead in her garage. She committed suicide at 28, and it hit many people pretty hard. From her suicide, it was clear that she was dealing with a lot of opposing feelings. After her passing, I laid on my blue suede couch, reading all of her social media posts and watching all of her videos. That the girl I knew in 7th-grade media studies class was gone.

Michelle's suicide hit me and others hard because she was a caring rebel. Now, I can't entirely make sense of her passing because I have no right to judge her decision. But from my research, it appeared that she was dealing with internal psychological trauma. Her mother battled with alcoholism, and she dealt with always healing others, but struggled internally. Breaking up with her boyfriend could have set off many time bombs. Again, I have no right to conclude someone's suicide.

I struggled with her death because Michelle was the second death within four months I had to process. One of my former students in my first class died at the age of 16, just four months before Michelle. The only stage of grief I paid attention to was avoidance.

I worked. A lot. I ignored my feelings and eventually, my body began to shut down. I got sick for at least six months. One week I had pink eyes, and the next week I got a UTI. I kept getting sick, and I worked and never took a break. It was only a matter of time that the avoidance of acknowledging death would make things worse.

Eventually, I lost my contract that was paying my bills. My body began to shut down even more. I stopped talking to people, and I stopped paying my bills. I was hiding. It was only a matter of time before I would have to face my financial fears. I was going to get kicked out of my apartment.

I replayed all the events that led me to this pink eviction slip. As I walked to my blue *Mini Cooper,* tears streaming down my face, the sharp pain moved like a dagger in my heart down to my gut—the feeling of paralysis, the disbelief that all pain would happen, was mind-boggling to me. Disoriented, I began plotting, devising some plan to figure out what move I should make next.

Suddenly, my internal feelings in my body turned into physical jolt. My face hit the steering wheel. Someone hit my car while I was in the park. My rear bumper dented, and I said to myself, 'I guess this is what it means to hit rock bottom.' Here I was, thousands of miles away from my family. I was embarrassed that I was someone who appeared to hit the black privilege lottery. Graduating from the right college, I made more money than my parents did when they were in their twenties. I appeared to look good on paper. I was embarrassed and prideful to ask for help and explain how I got to this point. All the while, I was also grieving and sad. I had to admit that pride got the best of me, and that pink slip of denial was a wake-up call.

That night, I slept on my friend's couch. All covered in dog hair. I didn't know what to do or who to talk to, so I turned to *Google* to help me find the answers. I typed in eviction and success.

An article from *Entrepreneur*[ii] about a guy who went from being fired, evicted, and became a millionaire by 30. While the insight seemed informative, I was turning 30 in three months, and the thought of being a millionaire didn't seem like it was an option.

I then typed up Black women and eviction. I found several articles about removal and success. There were two interesting articles:

1. Black women's eviction is higher than any race or gender According to the MacArthur Foundation[iii]

2. I found a local entrepreneur by the name of Ashley Fox, who talked about rising from being evicted to reclaiming her space after eviction.[iv]

I was slightly relieved. I found someone else who had similar experiences to me. As I sat there confused and unsure of different possibilities, I started to ask the question of how can I change my narrative around money and rebuild my future? That day, I wrote down that I was going to figure out my money for the next ten years. I started applying for waitressing jobs; I put my business on hold. I wrote out I will never be in a situation like this because I will take care of myself first.

Chapter 2
Debtors Anonymous

"Grief is about a broken heart, not a broken brain. All efforts to heal the heart with the head fail because the head is the wrong tool for the job. It's like trying to paint with a hammer—it only makes a mess. "[v]

— The Grief Recovery Handbook

Grieving can shake you to your very core. When you grieve, your brain tries to make sense of what went wrong. For me, my friends' suicide and running out of money made me rethink my entire existence. What skills do I have? How long do I have to live? Am I sane? My inner monologue drove me to feelings of defeat and insecurity. Shortness of breath would lead to crying on the floor. Sleeping on friend's couches became a regular occurrence. Grieving over something that was a loss proved to be the best decision that I made because I shed a part of me that no longer served a purpose. I was humbled, and I began to ask for help.

Asking for help was the most challenging thing I'd ever done. In my brain, asking for help meant that I was weak and couldn't take care of myself. I didn't want to bother my family because they also had financial difficulties. I began scrolling my *Rolodex*, looking for people to text for clarity. Fortunately, a friend of mine, Blake, was just the person I needed to speak to. I also trusted Blake's opinion because, in my eyes, I always wanted her black girl magic glow. Have you ever met someone who looks and smells like the money? That's how I felt with Blake. She smelled like it.

The next week I gave Blake a call. Blake, in all her magic, explained to me that the most significant life-changing program she participated in was Debtors Anonymous (DA). She explained to me that it helped her business and life grow. She had gone from having thousands of dollars of debt to a successful business. Blake explained to me that overnight success isn't real, and it takes a long time to truly master your money. Listening to Blake's money story provided me with a great rush of enthusiasm.

The next day, I attended my first DA phone meeting. Debtor Anonymous uses the principles of the twelve-step program of Alcoholics Anonymous, but they focus on debt. Twelve-step programs are straightforward and filled with a wide range of interesting people. When I first attended a Debtors Anonymous meeting, I hated it. I couldn't compute the steps. I kept calling in because I trusted Blake's advice. For months, I called the DA daily to listen to other people's experience and their shortcomings, never to share my own.

Dragging my feet for every DA meeting, I still called. Finally, one day I told people my money story. On a phone call, I told the group that I ran out of money, was sleeping on a dog-haired couch, and living thousands of miles away from my family.

The cathartic feeling telling my money story opened Pandora's box of possibilities. Once I told a group of people what happened, my inbox flooded with emails and texts of people trying to help. Many messages told me that it was entirely reasonable to hate the 12 steps. Some emails said to me that I needed to complete a financial inventory. The inventory involves breaking down the numbers behind my money. In addition to listening to daily DA calls, I would track every penny and forgive myself for feeling guilty about money. The release of financial awareness created a new purpose in my life, plus it was free!

As time progressed, I knew I needed a therapist because it was all too traumatic to deal with alone. But I didn't have much money to pay for one. My DA accountability partner helped me find affordable mental health care. Searching for free mental health was easy to come by because I lived in a city, but the waitlist was long. I decided to pay for *BetterHelp*. At that time, *BetterHelp* had a discounted rate based on your income.

Money and mental health are connected. When I lost money, I slipped into depression. My body would shut down. The vicious cycle would create a range of emotions, and I would feel guilty and ashamed of my actions. I would beat myself up for not doing a great job. I would get mad that I wasn't white, Beyoncé, or wealthy enough to get myself out of my money woes. And lastly, I would bury myself in overwork and make lists.

I realized that my identity as an African American woman created a subset of skills for resilience but suppressed my anxiety and depression. Resiliency is necessary because it emphasizes the positive factors of pushing through the face of adversity.[vi] This resiliency served me well throughout my childhood. But it created problems the older I got. Black women use resiliency as a badge of honor, but then we refuse to ask for help because it will pose us as weak. When I lost money, I had no clue who to ask for financial support. Neither of my parents had financial stability. It took a solid year for me to figure out that I could ask for financial and mental health help. I had to carefully find people that wouldn't judge me and understood my background.

The Network Map of My Financial BFFs

To rebuild my money story, I had to get real with my numbers. I would spend at least three hours a week figuring out how I could get out of my eviction mess. First, I organized all my old bills and previous tax-files. You name it, I pulled up old debts and started writing a list of them from largest to smallest. I purchased a filing cabinet so I could keep tabs on my bills and other materials. Money was a misunderstood element of my life; it became a game of finding financial savvy friends to new money patterns.

I had the exact ingredients for financial happiness, but I needed a chef to help me put together this economic pie. I needed Financial BFFs. A Financial BFF is an accountability group, friend, or financial support group that will help you with your money story without shame or guilt. For years, the only money advice I received from my family and my friends' parents was, *Pay down your student loans fast. Don't go to the check-cashing place for money. Pray about it. Break up with him because he makes no money.* The advice had good intentions, but I needed to find someone that wouldn't quote something out of a *BET* tv show.

I created a criteria list. 1) Must be a Woman of Color or 2) If they were white, they must know and understand the racial inequality and the word Allyship. Through A LOT of research, I found two financial best friends who would help me in this process. I know that's not for everyone, but I was able to let my guard down and made some changes quickly.

My first financial friend was an accountant, Erica Booth. Erica was an African American woman and became my shero. She helped me see the power of owning a business. My second financial best friend was a financial coach named Joe Holberg. Joe was unique because he was a teacher in inner cities. He was married to a Latinx woman, and he wrote a speech called Financial Justice. He had enough Allyship for me to get signed up for his program. I would schedule time with Joe to look at all my bills. Sometimes our talks were filled with me crying, but others were super positive. I became a seeker of all financial advice, in addition to my paid BFF options. I joined free money accountability groups like *Clevergirl Finance*, and I would attend Debtors Anonymous classes.

Lastly, to educate myself, I had to find financial bloggers and experts that looked like me or at least knew what the word inequality meant. I couldn't tell you how many times I'd read money books of folks that didn't represent who I was and what I cared for.

Chapter 3
Trying to Patch a Puzzle

Money awareness creates fertile ground for serendipitous run-ins. Here I was doing all the investigative work, and by design, I stumbled upon a financial site for women called *Daily Worth*. The *Daily Worth* is a website for mid-level career women. The founder of *Daily Worth*, Amanda Steinberg, had just released a book entitled *Worth it.* She explained her pitfalls and triumphs of marriage, divorce, kids, and the financial push to uncover her self-worth. I was able to see someone older than I was, trace back her steps as a teen, 20s, and 30s, and reverse her thoughts around money. It became my financial diet book; I began to put in my reps whenever I had the chance. I even attended one of her book tour events. There, she talked about her experience of hitting the reset button, her ups, and downs, but the key was to write out your money story.

Fired up from the interaction with the author, I purchased a small journal and entitled it as a money journal. My money journal used to gather thoughts around money. When my pen hit the paper, I knew I was creating an intimate relationship with myself and my money. I would describe my current relationships. I would figure out what I want in life. I would write about traumatic money incidents. When I wanted to explore the emotions of it, I would present the problems to my therapist. I was able to see my story for what it was and take my account in different directions. I was also able to heal and recover from events that occurred from the past.

Fear of Abandonment

I am recovering from what my therapist called fear of abandonment. Abandonment is a type of anxiety that people experience when they are continually concerned about losing someone or something. My childhood was relatively mild, but my teenage years were overwhelming. Writing in my money journal helped me unlock repressed feelings of self-doubt and insecurities. While writing this book, I was able to find a poem that I wrote.

You put the white coat on the table.

And you put it on yourself.

You try to fix what has been done to you,

But it seems to me that you don't have a clue.

But I see how you're feeling.

But I know all the destruction and pain.

You've got that feeling of destruction.

A feeling of self- release

You're trying to patch a puzzle.

You see, I'm not a poet; I loathe open mics. Growing up in the Bay Area, it is a rite of passage to appear bohemian. And my appearance as a Black Bay Area Bae, natural afro, and *Baby Gap* clothes gives off the vibe that I am woke. I'm even marrying someone who has written his thesis on James Baldwin, but I'm not that cool. In all my disdain of poetry, I wrote one poem, and it lives in my money journal. I would say that this is *Mr. Holland's Opus.* This poem was the story that I told myself on a daily basis. I was trying to make things perfect by ignoring emotions and trying to fix everything else but heal myself.

My "Ms. fix-it" personality began in high school. My high school years were filled with high expectations of succeeding. I attended a bougie school, one of the best in the state. But I was hiding my life. To provide you with a little more context, my mother used our family friend's address so I could attend. So, I would commute four cities over to go to the polished school in Walnut Creek, California, from my town of Bay Point, California. It was incredibly difficult because it felt like I was living two different lives. One life where I was always to be down with my People of Color counterparts in Bay Point. My other life, where I looked like the black extra on *The OC.*

I felt trapped in a web of an enigma. I couldn't tell people from my neighborhood, my struggles at my siddity school. I didn't tell people from my school about my friends from my community because they would think I was ghetto. As you can tell, that could be traumatic for a kid. I hid and listened to my indie sad girl music, but no one knew my pain, because I was an overachiever. 'You're black, you're strong,' I'd say to myself.

In addition to attending a school illegally, my fear of abandonment derived a series of events. My grandmother and great grandmother died within two months of each other during my sophomore year. A childhood friend of mine died because he was in the drug game. The guy I was always talking to on and off went and got another girl pregnant. It was all a hot mess. And the icing on the cake, both of my parents moved away from me. First, my father moved away to Long Beach to live with his mother because of his own money problems. Six months later, my mother moved to Houston, Texas, during my junior year because of a job transfer.

I felt that they had abandoned me at a time where I needed them the most. Both parents thought that my aunt would raise me for my last two years of high school and would keep a stable environment. Now, I know that's a lot to take it in. It was like a *Lifetime* movie in itself; my 16-year-old self couldn't handle it either. I felt like I'd lost everyone from my immediate family. I ignored my pain. No one knew that I was struggling because I told no one. I was the president of my school. I appeared to have it together, but I was struggling internally. It's still a topic I don't like to talk about, but they were defining moments of not feeling wanted.

My teenage years led me to my 20s with the constant feeling of insecurity and unworthiness. I struggled with being emotional with people. I didn't trust many people; I was also angry a lot. My distrust would lead to anxiety attacks. The anxiety attack would be sporadic, so I would never adequately address it.

When money problems would appear, I'd have anxiety attacks in the middle of the night, and I would be too embarrassed to talk about it. I'd regress to the 16-year-old girl I once knew, instead of the woman I'd become. I would avoid cash at all costs. On an ancestral level, I thought that I was exactly like my family with money. I would tell myself that I was terrible with it because my family was. I would say to myself 'what's the point of making more money if I'd lose it?' I created a downward spiral with my money story, and it took writing in the journal to see that. I would avoid looking at my money when times were tough. I was anxious about every aspect of my life.

My Childhood Self

My money journal also helped me figure out what my childhood dreams were. Through hours of work, I was able to figure out that 4th grade was a pivotal time for me. I got mooned. My pants fell off as I jumped off the swings. I got into my first and last fistfight. Someone had called me the N-word for the first time in my life. The most important piece about fourth grade was that I learned about the stock market. In Ms. Richardson's class, we picked three stocks: *Bank of America, Hershey's,* and *Atari* and followed them throughout the year. The stock would repeatedly go up and down. This experience was my first touch in finance, but I loved it.

I loved looking at financial evaluations through stocks. I loved learning about golf because my little elementary school brain thought that is where business deals were made. I loved researching the valuations of *Beanie Babies*, always questioning why someone would spend half of million dollars on the Princess bear. I wore blazers. I was able to see my childhood self: the good, bad, and the ugly. Skimming through old pictures and journals, and I realized that I love learning about money, and I was apparently good at math, even though I didn't feel like I was.

Through my money journals, I realized that not having the "gift of math" creates a detrimental issue in American culture. The most damaging problem of the "gift" mentality is that it makes people think we know who has the gift of math earlier. It also blocks many women from engaging with math at a young age. Stanford researcher Carol Dweck, who wrote *Is Math a Gift? Beliefs That Put Females at Risk*,[vii] explained the verbal weapon behind "gifted math people." Dweck says that our culture creates a "gifted" society too soon before understanding how people learn. Many adults believe that girls don't have the gift of math keeps them from pursuing those careers."[viii]

It took a crisis to figure out that I was good at math. It took me a long time to realize that I should take a deeper dive and maybe learn about money. Because money is math, I wanted to help others understand their money story. My money journal entries created the catalyst to apply to Financial Planning School and get my MBA. For both, I was able to get scholarships. I also was able to pay back all my undergraduate student loans. I became a financial wellness educator and taught budgeting courses to employees.

In my journal entries, I was able to see the future me. I recognized that I wanted to build a personal finance software that tackled some of the issues that I laid out in previous chapters. Many personal finance curricula don't tackle trauma or create a holistic approach. I hope to create the first personal finance national curriculum for the Department of Education.

Chapter 4
Ancestral Habits

It was a muggy day in my car. I was profusely sweating, waiting for the air conditioning to cool me down. As I sat there, I had a dilemma: should I listen to Drake's emo-rap and be in my feelings or nourish my brain? I chose the latter; I listened to *On Being with Krista Trippett,* [ix] and my life was changed forever.

Krista Trippett was interviewing researcher Rachel Yehuda. Yehuda and her research team at the Icahn School of Medicine wanted to know if people could inherit PTSD from their relatives. In Yehuda's research, they discovered that the descendants of people who survived the Holocaust have different stress hormones than their peers. From their research, descendants of the Holocaust would be more prone to anxiety disorders than their non- Holocaust peers. My jaw dropped. [x][xi]Can our relatives pass down their trauma to the next generation? How could I use this research to explain my anxiety? Does this translate to Women of Color? Deep down, I knew that my money story correlated to my mental health, but I didn't have the right vocabulary to explain it.

Every culture has experienced trauma, and I wanted to learn how our trauma can help us to understand disparities and how it affects our money stories. I began digging to find research. My overly ambitious self-became bamboozled by Yehuda's study. Scientists debunked the initial 2015 survey. Dr. Seema Yasmin, a journalist doctor, explained that the investigation had too small of a study size (32 people) to make broad claims.[xii] Damn! Although the research threw out the idea that trauma could pass down generationally, it still gave me a push to learn more about money and mental health.

One Coke to Rule them All

Like all families, mine had baggage and unspoken secrets. From Yehuda's study of generational PTSD, I began to get curious about my family. Do their patterns play a role in my thinking? The science behind my ancestral wounds started with a sandwich and a bottle of *Coke*.

I called my dad often on his lunch break. I always knew he was eating either Chinese food or a sandwich, always with a *Coke-a-Cola*. Because I knew the systems and routines of my dad, I began to wonder when he first began drinking Coke? Our conversation led to my yearlong study of habits.

"When did you start drinking Coke?" I asked.

"I've always liked it." my father replied

"But there must be something about it that makes you like it. Do you remember the first time you had a glass of Coke?

"Not really."

My fixation on finding out why my dad drinks Coke, lasted for a solid ten minutes until we uncovered the truth behind it. "Well, my first girlfriend's mom introduced me to them. I used to take her to the hospital every week, and every week she would reward me with a Coke. I think it made me feel close to home." At that moment, I understood how my dad felt. My dad's habit of Coke was formed by what Author Charles Duhigg likes to call the *Power of Habit.*[xiii] My dad's fascination with soda became a daily feedback loop in his brain to always drink soda during lunchtime. According to Duhigg, all feedback loops consist of three parts: a cue, a routine, and a reward. The Cue is a signal to tell you that you should be doing something. Routine is the act of creating a habit, and lastly, the Reward is the feeling you get after performing the task. My dad's 30+ year fascination with Coke habit occurred from a simple routine.

My dad's cue: Loraine's Mom needs something

Dad's Routine: My dad would take Loraine's mom to the hospital

Reward: Loraine's mom would buy my dad a Coke

Feeling attached: Feeling like he helped someone and that he belonged to a family

Thinking about my dad's fascination with Coke had me tripping. My family only drinks Coke! If people asked me what soda I preferred, I would say Coke, because of my dad's habit. I don't like any of them, but the sheer idea that addiction can turn into a family's origin story had me thinking. What if my patterns with money had to do with my family patterns? How could I use my family's habits to better understand my money story?

Ancestral Money Story

I am an only child born from Louisiana, and I grew up in California. Being born in the South and having Southern parents changed my perspective on living in California. We always had gumbo for Christmas, and when *Flat Stanley* traveled back to my school, he was topless and shimmering with Mardi Gras beads. I visited my relatives every summer as a tradition, so my family made sure that I wouldn't miss my Louisiana roots.

I started reaching out to extended family members while I was writing this book. I was mostly curious about my great grandmother, granny. I spent a lot of time with her when I was younger. She was and still is an essential part of my being. I can remember asking one of my Aunt Rita about my granny. Our conversation started small but opened up a can of Kunta worms for me.

Aunt Rita: *"You know, granny was strong. I'm not sure why grandpa would hit on her. You know, from time to time. There were a couple of times your dad when he was 13, would defend her. He would tell grandpa not to hit her. Your dad was quiet, but he cared. He took care of a lot of people at a young age."*

Me: *Do you think that's why he left the family at a young age?*

Aunt Rita: *Yeah, I think that's the left at 14 to California. I think he was sick of being responsible; I think he wanted to be a kid. He did a lot for mama and everyone because he was the oldest out of all of the grandkids.*

I was shocked that my aunt told me that my great grandmother was hit from time to time. But should I have been? At my church, I was brought up to believe that people that love their children should discipline them.

That famous Bible scripture in Proverbs "spare the rod and spoil the child." I remember getting whupped as a child. And my parents were pretty relaxed black folks. But the remnants of witnessing other people whupped as a way to raise children right was normal. The belief of corporal punishment internalizes in Black culture.

On a historical level, psychologists that lead communities of color talk about the racial disparities connected to spanking, corporal punishment, and practices of slavery. In *Spare the Kids: Why Whupping Children Won't Save Black America*, journalist Dr. Stacey Patton talks about how African-Americans adopted the method of spankings.[xiv] Patton explains that spanking and whuppings are attached to corporal punishment and reinforces racist ideology. In 2015, black children had the highest rate of abuse and neglect in their homes, according to the Department of Health.[xv] The unfortunate truth is that black children are more likely to be assaulted, seriously injured, or killed by a family member.

For years I thought that black children should be docile. Creating a narrative that black children are less civilized is commonplace. I can remember watching a family friend say that they would whup a kid like a runaway slave. The whuppin ideology isn't a cultural practice that Africans brought with them to this continent.[xvi] The trauma from slavery became a part of the practice. That night I had a lot to think about surrounding my choices and my family. I began to do some more digging. What was the feedback loop my family had? What makes spanking a child different from hitting a woman?

In the Black community, many of us had the belief that if a woman experienced abuse by a man, then she'd inflicted the pain on herself. To take this on a larger scale, two singers Rihanna and Chris Brown got into a violent altercation in 2009.[xvii] Brown was 19 years old at the time and beat up his girlfriend Rihanna and later pleaded guilty to felony assault. Many of my friends that were white canceled Chris Brown and stopped listening to his music. But my black friends, on the other hand, would have these long arguments of who was right or wrong.

Should we listen to Chris Brown's music after these altercations? Many of my friends believed that Rihanna was trying to keep a black man down. Some of my friends would justify Brown for hitting Rihanna because of ancestry; they would often say hurt people hurt people. Years later, we all found out that Rihanna and Chris Brown had dealt with abuse in their childhood. For a while, I stopped listening to Chris Brown, but I'm just as problematic as my friends. Years passed and I went back to singing "these hoes ain't loyal," and Chris Brown like it wasn't a thing. The fact is that if we justify assault as something that people do, then we have to go back to our habits and what we value.[xviii]

Drawing the dots back to my life, I started to look at how I viewed my relationships with my family. To be honest, I never regarded a man as someone who would help me. I didn't believe in marriage, and I thought that most men were abusive or liars. It didn't make any sense because I didn't have this problem from my father. He was like the mailman from *Mr. Roger's Neighborhood*. I know now why. With the help of a therapist, I had to come to terms that my ancestry led me to unusual habits to dating men. I dated men that were emotionally unavailable, nor was I. I didn't value romantic relationships because I didn't think that being in long-term relationships would last. It wasn't that I was exposed to violent men. But a lot of the women that I grew up around talked about how bad men were, how certain men couldn't be trusted. So, I didn't trust men.

Talking to my family brought a realization of what I felt as a black woman. How do my old habits play a role in my money habits? Through doing a lot of inner work I knew that the yearlong quest to figure out what exactly is the disconnect between communities of color and money. I knew I had a rare opportunity to share some of the connections to mental health, habits, and wealth.

Chapter 5
Adverse Childhood Experience

How we understand our emotions is one of the most powerful tools we possess, but it's also the most difficult. It's difficult because many of us don't recognize what we're doing until our brain matures. Even when our mind is mature, our past can affect us in the most unusual ways. Our emotions affect our money story because we have to see that our trauma can affect our spending.

Years ago, I was a second-grade teacher. It was the best teaching year of my life. One of the reasons why I enjoyed it so much was my talks with the kids. Standing at four feet, Langston, the second-grader, came to my class as a student who had been held back a year. Smiling from ear-to-ear, he came happy and ready to learn. I enjoyed my talks with Langston simply because I always felt that he was wise.

One day, Langston came up to me and told me that his "bad behavior" was in the past, and he told me that this year would be different. Langston and I had a bond because, like him, I repeated the second grade. As the year went by, I learned that Langston was diagnosed with ADHD and given medication. I also learned his story. His mother left while he was young and reappeared when he was six.

It occurred to many teachers that Langston had trauma and did not have the proper coping mechanisms. The ADHD appeared to be a side effect of instability in his life and learning. Now, I am not a doctor nor a psychologist, but I couldn't help wondering, how did Langston's trauma affect his life? How does it manifest through adulthood? Through the process of writing this book, it has occurred to me that unhealed trauma can be predetermined during childhood. And there is a term called the Adverse Childhood Experience (ACE).

Adverse Childhood Experience (ACE)

What if we could create a metric where we knew long term effects of adversity could determine our health and mental health outcomes?

All Americans have experienced adversity in their lives, but what if that trauma could affect our long-term mental health? The CDC and Kaiser started a study called Adverse Childhood Experiences (ACEs).[xix] The Adverse Childhood Experiences (ACEs) explains that someone's trauma or life experiences can link to long-term health and mental health outcomes. The study looked at adversity and provided a metric. Adverse Childhood Experiences Study (ACE Study) measured ten types of childhood adversity:

"Sexual, physical and verbal abuse, and physical and emotional neglect; and five types of family dysfunction. Based on a 1-5 metric. If someone has an ACE score of four or more, their life expectancy can change if not handled correctly."[xx]

Here's what we know from ACE:

- ⅔ of adults have at least one ACE[xxi]

- Thirty-six states and Washington, D.C. have done one or more ACE surveys. [xxii]

- The Adverse Childhood Experiences Study – the most extensive public health study you never heard of [xxiii]

- Championed in ACE research is California Surgeon General, Dr. Nadine Burke Harris. In her TED-Talk How childhood trauma affects health across a lifetime.[xxiv] Dr. Harris explains that doctors and therapists can understand the ACE scores and better assist their patients.

ACE scores can be traumatic and looking at a statistical number can seem intimidating. My ACE score is two. When I first saw the data, I panicked. But the more I researched, I realized that ACE scores could be a way of understanding your trauma. My ACE scores gave me superpowers, allowing me to beat my odds and get into a great university and a great career. My ACE scores were able to help me avoid a lot of problems in my life. The positive experiences in my early life can help build resilience. After a certain point, my resistance and my ACE scores were hindering my future self. I'm so grateful and privileged to figure out how I behave in a crisis, which my childhood self takes hostage.

If ACE scores can determine health scores, they have to explain how our money and mental health are connected. The most frustrating thing is that folks don't discuss the trauma around money, particularly in the finance community. We never talk about financial stress and its physical effects on our mental health. It's one of the least talked about topics in behavioral science. Most of the conversations are about investing and paying down your debt. All of those tips are fundamental, but when we're in a crisis, we fall back into old childhood patterns, regardless of our socioeconomic status. There is always Lil trauma following us wherever we go. Sometimes we remain unaware of the injury that we don't recognize because it's normalized. So, even simple things like grocery shopping can bring up a trauma because your parents said that they didn't have enough money in the bank to pay for food. Unconscious beliefs lay dormant, and it's up to us to unlearn some of the past to create a better future.

The unfortunate thing is that we don't have a money and mental health policy group in the United States to tackle this thing firsthand. But there are positive steps being made in the right direction. Across the pond, the U.K. has a Money and Mental Health Policy organization that looks at folks' mental health conditions and figures out their spending habits. [xxv]It's helpful for us because many of the studies involved can be duplicated here in the states.

In the U.S. we are making some changes to create fiscal policy around consumer finance. Thanks to Senator Elizabeth Warren and her team in 2008, The Consumer Financial Protection Bureau (CFPB) is an agency that provides tools for people to understand their spending habits.[xxvi] The agency mostly handles folks who are having to deal with financial hardship, but this is crucial because if we can see problems in spending in an unbiased way, we can look at preventive methods. Hopefully, with the data from the CFPB, we can form a money and mental health policy group.

Tulsa Oklahoma

The state of Oklahoma ranks No. 1 in the nation's childhood trauma, according to a 2017 National Survey of Children's Health.[xxvii] The U.S. Census Bureau found that Oklahoma children incurred two or more adverse experiences. [xxviii]The positive aspect of this terrible statistic is that the state is trying to understand how adults have these problems and how to reverse these problems for children. A special report from *Tulsa World*, entitled *Breaking the Cycle*, analyzes the science behind ACE scores in Tulsa and finds ways to help Oklahomans suffering from the problems and address them appropriately.[xxix]

What caught my eye from this study was how soda, cigarettes, and trauma were all connected to childhood experiences. As it turns out, your ACE scores can cultivate unhealthy habits as soothing mechanisms. Things like smoking cigarettes, overeating, soda, or any addiction can help regulate when you're stressed. Jennifer Hays-Grudo director for The Center for Integrative Research on Childhood Adversity (CIRCA) in Tulsa explained that habits form to solve a more serious problem; the problem is that as a child or adult, you haven't regulated your emotions.[xxx] CIRCA and public service specialists are developing evidence-based programs to prevent and intervene with ACEs within Oklahoma.

In the last chapter, I talked about how my dad has a habit of drinking Coke. Like we mentioned earlier, my father witnessed and defended his grandmother while his grandfather was in the act of abuse. He moved to California as a 14-year-old in search of a better life. Looking at my dad's soda addiction, I was able to see how it was a coping mechanism. My dad slowly limited his

Coke intake from every day to occasion after our conversations and a few trips to the doctor. Seeing how all of our habits and behaviors are so intertwined, I was able to understand a little more about my dad.

Am I ready to embark on learning the trauma on my mother's side? I think I would need more therapy and wine for that.

Chapter 6
Women of Color

I chose to write a book about Women of Color because I've always been in awe of Women of Color, but I've never seen that much representation of them within personal finance. There are Women of Color trailblazers like Marsha Barnes, Brittney Castro, or Kristin Wong that are leading the way. Still, in comparison to the wider population, our representation isn't the entire WOC population. I was tired of seeing the same statistics of Women of Color not achieving wealth or financial stability over and over again. I wanted to know more about it, so during my time as an MBA and a Certified Financial Planner student, I decided to research more about financial systems and what are disbarring Women of Color to get the shorter end of the stick.

There is a wealth gap behind race and gender, and historically Women of Color have always been given the shorter end of the stick. It's frustrating because Women of Color are just as capable as any other group to build wealth and create financial stability but are not taught the basics. It is simply not enough to address income gaps or budgeting, there are hundreds of books that address that, but we need to get a bird's eye of historical discrimination. Creating a bird's eye view is crucial because many of us get frustrated with ourselves and get mad at our parents. But there are a lot of barriers that created discrimination far before we were born. Until we recognize how they influence us, we cannot fully process the ideas around our money and reach our full potential.

In this portion of the book, we're talking about the historical money story of Women of Color. We're looking at four racial identities: Native, Latinx, African, and Asian American women. When I thought about writing this book just for African American women, I had nightmares. I kept feeling as if there were multiple women in all different colors speaking to me and asking me to tell their story. So, I started asking 40 Women of Color to tell me about their money story.

Next, I looked at the history of American Culture. And saw how the problems from the past have affected our futures. What I noticed is that a lot of policies were in place to create a negative narrative around Women and Color and their money habits. For each chapter, I wanted to gain an understanding of what the barriers were that could keep Women of Color back. As you've seen in my story, there were a lot of scenarios that created my abandonment anxiety, and it was the culprit of me feeling small and not worthy. There were a lot of cultural elements that described my habits, behaviors, and beliefs.

Since I identify as a black woman, this perspective is written from a black woman's point of view; however, over two years, I've researched and conducted interviews with forty women. There were patterns of ancestral trauma in each conversation, and it made sense to explore why people were dealing with their problems in the way that they were.

The political discourse of the term Women of Color is controversial. Some folks love the term, and some people hate it. It makes sense because the term Women of Color is a political one. The name, Women of Color, can create a US vs. White America conversation. It can dismiss Black, Latinx, Native, and Asian-Americans' experiences and puts it all into this ONE experience. In the preceding chapters, we will discuss the experiences of different cultures separately.

Women of Color are amazing women that are continuously defying all odds. Most of the women I spoke with identified as college-educated. Around two-thirds of the interviewees made more money than their parents made. I hope that although some of the content could be traumatic, you see how each individual was able to tell their story to help you the reader and help me heal.

Chapter 7
Historical Money Story of Asian Americans

Cindy's Story

Living in all four time zones in the US, Cindy had a unique experience learning about other cultures and herself, becoming a writer, editor, and actor. Nerding out to all things cinema, it's no wonder you'd catch Cindy podcasting and claiming her nerdiness far and wide. Cindy was a 20 something, making it as a freelancer and living in New York City. Her mother had always taught her the power of savings, and Cindy believed those skills helped her to become a good Asian daughter.

"I am a saver. I always have been when I was younger; my mother gave me an allowance, and a small portion of that allowance has gone into saving. So, as I got older, I followed the same instructions as what my mom told. I have money saved, I invest a portion of my investment accounts, and I spend the rest. My mother

always taught me that no one would help you with your money, so you have to take care of yourself because no one will. I also look at my friends that are always talking about being broke, but they don't save, and I do worry for them, but I'd like to stop spending money on avocado toast."

Cindy was proud of her upbringing, and her mother prepared her to survive the high cost of living in New York. As the conversation with Cindy progressed, I knew that there was something that she wasn't sharing. There was. There was a strong sense of guilt from her taking care of herself financially. I asked her if any questions occurred with the money that concerned her. She said that there was a strong sense of guilt with her mom and grandmother.

"My grandmother was in a Japanese internment camp in the US, and she had land, and the government took her property and put her in an internment camp. I asked my mom to talk more about it, but I know that it would be too much. I know that my family carries around fear—the fear of not having anything. My family had land and lost their homes during WWII and lived in an internment camp. I try to honor my grandmother. I think some of the patterns are drawbacks to my grandmother. You know I haven't purchased glasses in two years. I know that it's not that bad, but I need to check my prescription, but I'm so scared to spend my money."

Cindy was dealing with her family's trauma. During WWII, her family lived in the United States during the Exclusionary Act. To make matters further complex, Cindy's family was Japanese, and her family lost everything and were incarcerated during WWII. It's important to note that Cindy was taking care of her finances, but her family was dealing with a scarcity mindset. Imagine how you'd feel if your family lost their financial stability in such a short time?

Asian Americans were pivotal in building America's economy, but Asian Americans had a tough time becoming citizens in the United States for the first hundred years of migration. This blockade of citizenship affected opportunities for Asian American's Money Story.

In the 19th Century, Filipino, Chinese, and Japanese migrated to the United States to find jobs. Chinese Immigrants moved to the West to work on railroads during the Gold Rush. Japanese immigrants moved to Hawaii to work in the Sugarcane fields.[xxxi] Filipino immigrants moved to Louisiana as hunters and trappers, but for decades Filipinos were considered "silent occupants in the US. The US government wanted to occupy the Philippines, so there was a different agreement surrounding Japanese and Chinese immigrants. The migration benefited American businesses because Asian immigrants were cheap labor.

As Asian cultures moved into the United States, new beliefs of race identity began to plague the conversation. Pioneering in race identity pseudoscience was Dr. Samuel George Morton. Dr. Morton wrote the *Types of Mankind*, which was an in-depth study regarding race biology. Race biology is the belief that there is a hierarchy of the best race, based on brain size.[xxxii] In *Types of Mankind*, the premise was that Chinese and non- whites are lesser beings.[xxxiii] News publications and political propaganda stirred "'race science," and American citizens started believing that Chinese immigrants were less than human. This anti-Chinese, and later anti-Japanese and was bound to turn into American policy. Legal action soon followed.

The first notable legal documentation occurred in 1882. The Chinese Exclusion Act was the first significant law restricting Chinese immigration into the United States. Signed by President Arthur, the Act declared that the Chinese were ineligible for citizenship and created a block for Asian migration in the United States.[xxxiv] The Exclusion Act was renewed for another ten years, making it illegal for Chinese Americans to legally enter the United States.

The US eliminated and stopped Chinese and Japanese migration for over 70 years. For decades, Chinese Americans and others from the Asian Diaspora couldn't receive citizenship, mainly through the use of the Chinese Exclusion Act. [xxxv]

It wasn't until 1943 that Congress repealed the Exclusion Act, and not fully practiced until 1965.[xxxvi] While President Franklin Roosevelt signed the repeal, he also created an executive order in 1942 to place Japanese descents in isolated camps during World War II. [xxxvii]The Immigration Act of 1965 officially allowed Asian Americans the ability to immigrate to the United States and be citizens legally.

You're probably wondering, how does this affect the current landscape of Asian Americans in the United States?

Asian Americans were limited to their land and retrieved citizenship. Remember how we said in 1942 the Exclusion Act repealed? That is the age of your grandma; chances are, if they are Asian, Americans are having a hard time with retirement. Asian American families have a significant reliance on public cash assistance, of poverty over white families. Asian Americans have a high risk of financial insecurity. One-in-seven Asian Americans over the age of 65 live in poverty. [xxxviii]Some argue that Asian Americans live with their grandparents, but being a senior citizen has a lot of funds going into hospital visits, long term care, etc. Relying on funds puts a financial strain on family financial relationships.[xxxix]

Drawing back to Cindy's Story it was clear that although her grandmother experienced her land being taken away it has passed down two generations. Like we've mentioned before, our family's trauma can affect us in the most peculiar ways. Cindy's family experience provided her with stability, but also at the same time scarcity.

Chapter 8
Asian American Women's Money Story

Before we dive into the realness of Asian American Women's Money Story. It's important to note that in a short period, a portion of Asian American Women are killing the game. According to Pew Research, Asian Americans are considered to have the highest income out of all the ethnic groups and that Asian women make more money than white women in income.[xl] Asian women are dominating college life. It is something to celebrate and highlight.

It's also important to note that we have a conflict because, in America, we place all Asians into one category of Asians. That's a lot of different ethnicities into one monolith group. This US Census includes around sixteen different ethnic groups, including Chinese, Japanese, Indian, Thai, Southeast Asian cultures, and so many more. In the portion of the Asian American Story, we break down some of the current conflicts within the Asian American Community. We'll look at Saving Face, the

Model Minority Myth, and redefining high income. We'll briefly talk about these current conflicts and see how it plays a role in the ongoing money story.

Saving Face

In college, I joined an international club at UC Berkeley. And within this organization, 80% percent of the members were Asian. There was one other black person aside from me, and even she was half Black and Chinese (fluent too)! One of the many topics that would cross the conversation table frequently was the concept of Saving Face.

Saving Face is a social value that Asian cultures share. Asian American families focus on honoring their family first, and in return, the goal for an individual is to avoid humiliation at all costs and not disdain the family's name and reputation. Many of my friends who were dealing with their identities had a very different dilemma than I did during college. They were constantly questioning their decisions: Do I follow my American friends and "follow my heart?" Or do I go to college and follow my parent's wishes and attend law or medical school?

Going back to many of the interviews I recorded, like Cindy's Saving Face struck a chord in everyone's ethos. All the interviews would explain how Saving Face was a core value in their families' money stories. Now, the tricky part is that if someone disrespected their family, it would be a hot mess. This ideology is different from Western culture, which is to honor yourself, aka self-care is very different from another culture. These ideas can definitely affect your values. And the future. Can it affect the way Asian American women handle leadership? Could Saving Face affect gender roles?

Julie was a high powered Asian American woman who worked in Wall Street and had a successful day trading business but was consistently dealing with the inner conflict of male domination and who controls sexual power. When I began speaking with her, she explained to me that her father was someone who used infidelity and abuse as a form of power. Julie was in her 40s, and she told her tremulous relationships with men.

"My father abused my family, and my mom stuck with the abuse. He used money as a mode of waving it over our family, and to "save face," my mother dealt with the infidelity and the abuse until she decided that it was enough. I repeated the pattern, but no one could tell because I was put together."

For Julie, Saving Face was the more extreme side. Here, Julie's father used the money to keep Julie's family in a difficult bond. The family was willing to Save Face and avoid divorce. Her pattern was internalized from her parents and eventually played throughout her life.

Model Minority Myth

"This has affected me because people have certain assumptions about my intellect which isn't necessarily bad, but Minority myth includes the idea that Asians don't rock the boat & go along essentially with white American culture & I def don't fit that at all"- Jessica, 28

The stereotype of all Asian Americans being superior students started as a way to create conflict between African American Americans. During the Civil Rights Movement, the *New York Times* published an article entitled Success Story, *Japanese American Style.* In so many words, the article was the first of many to create a myth that all Asian Americans are geniuses. The article stated that Asian Americans are a "group who have achieved a higher level of success than the general population." This one size fits all model forces Asian students to be surrounded by an unrealistic expectation of being the best in academics. It also was a way of putting Asian Americans against African Americans. The Model Minority Myth was a way to say that Asian Americans are above other Black and Latinx communities.

When I spoke to Lisa, a biracial Asian American Student, she had the unique experience to explain that it excludes Asian Americans to fend for themselves.

"The Minority Myth limits a child's growth in school because the teacher and staff give less attention to an Asian student under the assumption that they are "fine" and don't need extra help because they are "inherently smart." It can also make the child warier to ask questions and seek help because they are also pressured by the stereotype that they shouldn't need help."

As Lisa explains, Asian nationalities divide races and create a lot of pressure to learn the best.[xli] It also ignores the history of racism in the United States towards Asian Americans and says if you are smart, you can make money easily, ignoring struggles as other minorities and that is simply not true.

Income does not Mean Wealth

The notion that Asian American women all are financially stable isn't factually true. Pew research explained that Asian American Women are the highest-paid group and are doing better than every ethnic group and aren't taking into account several factors that lead to a lot of confusion.

First, let's talk about the boost in Income. Income is the amount that people receive on a regular basis.[xlii] Wealth is the length of time "that a person could maintain their current lifestyle without receiving compensation for As we've mentioned before, Asian Americans were not granted citizenship until 1943. Around the same time that your grandma was a teen. So many Asian Americans born in America did not have the opportunity to build wealth over generations.

Secondly, the idea that all Asians are high earners is a dangerous claim. If we break down income based on ethnicities, we come up with large inequality gaps. According to Prosperity Now, Hmong, Cambodian and Laotian Americans have "high poverty rates of about 38%, 29%, and 18.5%, respectively."[xliii] In New York, some Asian populations are the poorest in the entire region of New York City. When we break down what days are equal payday, we're lumping all ethnicities into one pot and assuming that they are all the same.

Lastly, we must break down how wages are situated. For many Asian women, there is a giant hourglass of income allusion. When we look at Asian Americans, we look at all incomes and create an average based upon them. A lot of Asian Americans including Indian, Japanese, and Chinese, are coming to America with high paying jobs. If you break it down, nationality has the biggest inequality gaps within the United States. According to EQPD, "Vietnamese women earn $.64, Hmong women earn $.57, and Burmese women earn only $.50. Creating "they all earn good money" rhetoric doesn't really help communities grow.[xliv]

How does it affect Asian American Women Money Stories?

"People also use it to say we're richer than white people but we don't hold more leadership roles than them, we don't own as much property or wealth as them, & when things like the coronavirus happen, all of that goes out the window & we become the Yellow Peril and we're crazy."

- Lisa

The myth of being the best Asian American can dramatically affect Asian American emotional health and well-being.[xlv] In a recent article, Mental Health Among Asians- Americans, Doctoral Candidate, Koko Nishi, MA collected a series of data and found that mental health around Asian Americans is few and far between, but when data has been collected the results found were staggering. The National Latino and Asian American Study (NLAAS) "found that Asian Americans have a lot of health pressures, but did not seek out for help Asian Americans are three times less likely to seek mental health services than Whites."[xlvi]   So, not only are you supposed to maintain a perfect image of academic success, but you must never talk about it. With pressures of Saving Face has a strong role in people's money stories.

Chapter 9
African American Historical Money Story

Nia, Sade, and I had a 2-hour phone call. I was talking to two successful women in their 30s: Nia, a black doctor from Houston, Texas, and Sade, a public policy specialist in New York. Nia talked about her existence as a black woman and money.

"My biggest issue with moving forward is figuring out what stories I keep telling myself and ignoring red flags. Because black folks have taken so many roles that we forget who we are. Many of us talk about trauma, but that is all of our stories. Many of us lead with our trauma stories. Being Black, everyone has dealt with racism, and because I identify with my blackness with my narrative, I only celebrate the rags to riches stories. Black people have their struggle moments, but the problem is that I am ignoring my standards and my future standards because I'm dwelling on my past.

Toxic masculinity and money go hand and hand, and I was dating someone who had made it. The guy I was dating grew up dirt poor and managed to get into UPenn for his MBA. He had a lot of trauma and wasn't dealing with it. I was so impressed with his money story, but he didn't respect me as a woman, but I was so attracted to his rags to riches story and that he had "made it" that ignored things that were not acceptable."

Sade: *"I agree with you. I've been so focused on the struggle that I was dating someone for two years that he didn't work on himself at all. His family praised him like he was God's gift to earth because his other brothers didn't have a good job. Because I kept saying this guy has endured so much as a black man, I wasn't paying attention to his actions. I think we've black women who are programmed to survive trauma porn. Trauma porn means we are addicted to traumatic stories surrounding black people. We live in trauma. I am living in fear. But if you talk to Becky, who's lived in the suburbs, lives her life and just watched 'Get Out,' she doesn't have the same traumatic experience. But it's like I'm doing the work, but focused on Trauma porn, and everyone is addicted to it."*

Trauma is at the core of the African- Americans ethos. From being considered as property during slavery to police brutality. African Americans have experienced economic discrimination and dehumanizing a culture and black identity. To truly understand the historical money story, we must look at our first touch of financial independence after slavery.

The Freeman Bank

The African American money journey began after the Emancipation Proclamation. After the Civil War, the Lincoln administration wanted to create a bank for African Americans soldiers to save their wages. The administration debated several ways they could usher free blacks into the economic society. [xlvii]

In 1865, minister and abolitionist, John W. Alvord, met with business leaders and philanthropists in a series of negotiations for black soldiers.[xlviii] Alford noticed that many regions were creating savings accounts for soldiers, and he wanted to create a more unified banking system for black soldiers. Word had caught, and the surge of banks created an organization called the Freedman Bank.

Between 1865 and 1871, the Freedman's Bank opened thirty-seven branch offices in seventeen states and the District of Columbia. [xlix] In less than a decade, more than fifty-seven million dollars were deposited, as well as 70,000 depositors and open accounts. When it comes to building incomes, it's important to note that creating a race-specific bank turned out to be problematic.

When President Lincoln signed the Freedman Saving and Trust Company, there was a clear objective. A simple savings institution created primarily for former slaves and their descendants. Never built wealth over time. Operationally, the bank operators didn't have a strategy to expand black banking. [l]For the first six years, the president of the Freedman bank was white. At that time, the president invested the money into unsecured stocks, bonds, Treasury notes, or other securities of the United States.

Also, it turns out that the Freedman Bank used its limited assets to loan funds to non-African Americans, and according to the Freedman Legacy Project, was making several especially risky investments across industries in the process. [li]

In 1873, Seneca Sandstone Company received approval for an unsecured loan by a bank board member, Henry D. Cooke.[lii] The owner of the Sandstone Company and its board members were white. A financial panic in 1873 stuck in the United States, the quarry loan fell into default, and depositors and the president of the board made Fredrick Douglas the bank director. When Douglas found out about Seneca, he desperately attempted to stabilize the bank and even invested $10,000 of his own funds. But sadly, later that year, the bank was terminated.[liii]

A Congressional investigation of Henry D. Cooke was mandated, but Black people did not receive any of the money that they had saved. [liv]Congress explained 62% of depositors would recover their money, but the black depositors never did.[lv] Like the promise for 40 acres and a mule, black people saved their money only to find it had disappeared before their eyes. It turns out that black people were good at saving money but barred from investing.

Some folks will say, "well, this happened a long time ago," but let me put it under a personal lens. My great aunt is 98 years old. Her mother was a sharecropper. If we look at her life, the fallout from the Freedman Bank was only two lifetimes ago. More importantly, though, that's two/three financial life cycles of wealth growth and accumulation and decades of compounding that never got started.

Black Wall Street

In the early 1900s, the African American community wanted to create a black-owned bank experience. In the late 19th and early 20th century, there were 57 black-owned banks.[lvi] Depending on the scale of the Great Depression, that determined how long a bank stayed in motion. The most notable banks within the community were the Black Wall Street in Tulsa, Oklahoma.

During the late 1880s, America was re-allocating Native Americans' land through the Dawes Act. An African American landowner, O.W. Gurley purchased 40 acres of land in Tulsa. [lvii] The Greenwood district became the mecca of Black Capitalism. During this time, the KKK was very prevalent within the community. Despite discrimination and Jim Crow laws, black shops were thriving. Black-owned businesses fostered, theaters, schools, and social health. [lviii]The city had more than 10,000 African American residents.[lix]

An accusation of sexual assault dramatically changed the outcome of the community. On May 30, 1921, the charge began with 13-year-old Dick Rowland. Rowland went in an elevator with 17-year-old Sarah Page.[lx] When the elevator doors opened, Sarah Page screamed, and Rowland ran away. Nothing happened, and Sarah Page did not press charges against him, but Rowland was arrested anyhow and put in jail. That information was just enough for Ku Klux Klan members to get the "justice" that Sarah Page needed.

On May 31, 1921, within "16 hours, police had arrested 60% of Black residents living in Black Wall Street".[lxi] Bombs dropped on the Greenwood district. No man, woman, or child was safe. In two short days, the growing community was in ruins. Many of the buildings burned to the ground. The *Red Cross* estimates that 1,256 houses burned down; 215 others looted.[lxii] No one knows the true number of deaths that took place, but the forecast is around 300 people. When the news broke loose about Tulsa's incidents, the media called it a riot. The truth is, Black Wall Street is a massacre on American soil. Just hours after the massacre, the police dropped all charges on Dick Rowland. "The police concluded that Rowland had most likely stumbled into Page or stepped on her foot."[lxiii] A crumbling of a society from a slip is the American ethos of identity.

How does this play into African American Money Story?

The black historical money story has a lot of positive areas. African Americans are savers and investors, despite hundreds of years of oppression. Of course, we are nowhere near equity, but the hope is that these stories should be a constant reminder that we are more than capable of saving, but historically have gotten the short end of the stick. We have to undergo the belly of ancestral trauma and wounds.

Chapter 10
African American Women Money Story

African American Women are creating their seat at the table. The number of businesses owned by black women grew by a stunning 164% between 2008-2018.[lxiv] Building businesses are a catalyst for building upward mobility. With the boost in business, black women must understand and address some of the policies and factors that prevent financial stabilization, so that building business can thrive. In this portion of the book, we talk about the incarceration and Post Traumatic Slave Syndrome.

Incarceration

"Every black man I know has been in contact with the law, even my minister. So, in my mind, no man is safe. My boyfriend is African, and I told him that he would come in contact with the law. My youngest son's dad is in jail, and I've seen how that affects him. His first felony

occurred when he was 16, he struggles with getting an apartment, and he has to take minimum wage jobs." - Lisa

When I spoke to Lisa, a single mother, and a financial coach, she talked about how every black male in her life has interacted with prisons or jail. Like Lisa, Black women have to continually deal with incarnation at a higher rate than other cultures. It would be an injustice not to acknowledge that the prison systems affected black families as a whole in America. According to the NAACP, the incarceration rate of African Americans is five times the rate of a white person.[lxv] The sentencing project explained that one out of three black men would go to prison at least once in their lifetime. The Sentencing Project said that the Black Women's imprisonment rate is twice as high as white women between 1980- 2000, but this has since declined dramatically.[lxvi]

As a black woman, it took me a while to realize how interconnected the prison is in the black community. I had a couple of cousins that were "on vacation," but were actually serving time in jail. There are several policies, and that leads to a high incarceration rate. For the brevity of this book, we will talk about sentencing through Kemba's Smith court case.

In 1994, Kemba Smith was charged for illegal drug activities and sentenced to 24.5 years in prison. [lxvii]Kemba did not have a criminal record but was dating a drug dealer who was FBI's most wanted, and to make matters worse, she was seven months pregnant. Smith's recalls her scenario to the American Commission on Human Rights: [lxviii]

"I did not traffic in drugs, but I knew my boyfriend did. I knew while living with him that he did not have a job, and we were living off of the proceeds of his drug

crimes. I never claimed total innocence, and this is the reason why I pled guilty."

Smith served six years of her prison sentence and was then pardoned by the Clinton Administration. Kembra was not only involved with a drug dealer, but she was in an abusive relationship, and her real relationship was not disclosed in the US court case.[lxix] Smith was a unique case, but it shows how sentencing can affect a whole family dynamic. Her son was unable to be raised by his mother and had to be raised by his grandparents instead. Kembra was charged for a crime that did not involve her in any of the activities. So, that affected her ability to achieve financial stability.

What is interesting to note is that once Kembra was released, she completed college, and graduated law school. She is now a business owner fighting for women in domestic violence and women imprisonment. Kembra had the opportunity to create a seat at the table, but so many others don't have that chance.

Mental Health

It would be unjust not to acknowledge that to be a Black woman requires resilience. But with that resilience, the question remains; when do Black women have time to heal? I would argue that we hustle more than most people. African American women and the feelings of confidence and self-worth are always deep-rooted within our minds and hearts. As our identities are continually asking for more, we are still affected by impressions from the past. Black women have been taught to be strong and not show feelings. Well, unless you're at church and the spirit hits.

There is always a mental health component to all money, and this self-worth affects our psyche. There is a significant push for equality, but until we have a full-on conversation about how we view ourselves to white America, we will never be able to sit at the table because some don't think we deserve a seat. That is the most uncomfortable pill to swallow. This awkward feeling could be known as Post Traumatic Slave Syndrome.

Post Traumatic Slave Syndrome (PTSS) is a theory that describes survival behaviors in the African American community and the Diaspora.[lxx] Coined by Dr. DeGruy, PTSS is a condition that explains behavior patterns from slaves and their descendants.[lxxi] DeGruy explains that black people have to deal with America's unconsciousness. The racist ideologies that African Americans are inherently or genetically inferior to whites. Black people internalize the feelings of inferiorities in comparison to whites.

Post Traumatic Slave Syndrome creates a strong sense of hopelessness and anger. This hopelessness is valid; between how people view your name or what neighborhood you've grown up in, black people are scrutinized from top to bottom.[lxxii] And the feelings of always having to compare oneself to White culture is draining. If we look at multigenerational trauma, we've adapted familiar behavior that we aren't consciously aware of. There are 300 years of oppression without studying the impact of stress that it was on the black psyche.

In all honesty, the PTSS approach is tricky to face because it raises a lot of questions for our identity and feelings. It was difficult to admit that I felt inferior, I had to admit this to myself to move past it. I can tell you about the inequalities it shows blacks have experienced, but that would make an entire book. What we need to know is where we stand, young folks are not addressing all these different forms of racism and discrimination. When I talked to my closest friend, a black sociologist, Zoe, we had a heated discussion, which included a lot of clap backs. Zoe had qualms with the theory because it wasn't tested in many sample size groups. There hasn't been any clinical research around it, so it's also why many people can dismiss the argument.

Why is this important for Black Women's Money Story?

As mentioned in the conversation with Sade and Nia, trauma porn affects black women's money story. Black women, in particular, are hyper-aware of discrimination. And black women are hustling hard, but we have some internal healing to address our self-worth. Despite the Civil Rights reforms, there is still an unconscious bias towards black women retrieving equity. Where we stand for every dollar that a white male makes, Black women are paid .$61women to meet that dollar-based on ACS Census data for a black woman to meet.[lxxiii] Understand the trauma that many of us have endured is in the collective. If Black women feel inferior to others or consistently have to fight because black women aren't taking care of themselves first, they will neglect their future growth.

Chapter 11
Native American Historical
Money Story

The Historical Money Story of Native Americans has a unique positioning in the United States identity. There are over 562 federally recognized tribes in the U.S.[lxxiv] Native Americans represent 1.8% of the population but have a legal and financial situation that is complex and deserves justice.[lxxv] Not a lot of people talk about Native American culture unless you see commercials about casinos or protests. There is so much beauty in ancestry, and as your brief guide, I hope that I can paint an accurate picture of money and mental health.

Imagine a world where you receive eviction notices. You keep paying bills on time, but the owner wants you out of the house. They put out a noise complaint because you have one wine party that goes on for way too long. The owner changes their agreement from annually to a month by month, and you are outraged. You ask your family to help pay lawyer fees, and your family agrees, but the lawyer fees are just too much, so eventually, you cave in and move somewhere else. As a nation, we have consistently given an eviction notice to Native Americans.

The first set of eviction notices began once Columbus came into the neighborhood. Each eviction notice started small, but as a whole, the ultimate goal for the federal government was to own Native American land legally. The search for creating separate but equal laws began in the 1820s with President Jackson.[lxxvi]

In 1828, President Jackson wanted to purchase land for private equity and crafted a federal policy to retrieve the unclaimed property.[lxxvii] For the first time in history, nation policy encouraged the removal of "dominant federal Indian Policy."[lxxviii]

In the winter of 1831, President Jackson gave the Native American tribes a pink slip. The Indian Removal Act of 1830 drafted to convince tribes to move from their land, into the west of the Mississippi. Tribes, including Choctaw and Cherokee, fought against the American government.

The Cherokee brought Jackson's Administration to court in the case of *Worcester v. Georgia (1838)*. The Supreme court favored the Cherokees, but Jackson's Administration denied the court's decision. In 1838, Cherokee and Choctaw tribe were "bound in chains and marched in double file" to new Indian territory.[lxxix]

The Jackson Administration boasted and called this battle as the Trail of Tears because as Indian tribes were forced out of their Southeastern homes, they left a trail of blood and death as they moved into the new location. Many people did not survive the trip, and overall, it is estimated that 15,000 died from the relocation. [lxxx]*Trail of Tears* forced people out of their homes to a new land.

As a result of the Trail *of Tears*, the government created more laws for relocation. In February of 1887, the Cleveland Administration approved a bill that allowed a breaking up of reservation land in the Dawes Act. [lxxxi]The bill forced Native Americans to re-register on a "tribal roll" that granted lands. Many Indians that received property didn't have the necessary supplies to farm. The allotments turned out to be a way to put tribes in conflict with each other, allowing men to own the land. Some tribes did not have the same treatment. Cherokees, Creeks, Choctaw, Chickasaws, and Seminoles as the "five Civilized Tribes," so they favored land more than other tribes. Many tribes did not have the legal right to receive the property.[lxxxii] If tribes had an area, they didn't have the money or proper supplies to farm.

Even though Native Americans have acres of land, they don't truly own it. It's explained that Native Americans are "Land Rich Dirt Poor" means, but tribes don't control natural resources.[lxxxiii]

Identity- Race Relations

The identity of Native Americans as a race is an awkward conversation. Legally, Native Americans are not a "minority group." There is not a single definition of Indian or Native American as a race. [lxxxiv]Tribes have criteria for being Native American and undergo a process called blood quantum.

The U.S. The Department of Interior created the Blood Quantum to determine whether Americans qualify as Native Americans or belong to a tribe. Similar to a voter's card, the Certified Degree of Indian Blood is a certification that shows what the tribe has tribal blood.[lxxxv] The Blood certification is a calculation given by a government or tribal official. The goal for the program was to document if an individual had a card, but the caveat was that the individual must have full blood quantum.

Many people who were drafting the blood quantum team, all had subjective ways of explaining who was full blood and who wasn't. The people who created the quantum field of blood didn't know the communities, because they were government officials or the tribal negotiators were biased.[lxxxvi] Elizabeth Rule, a doctoral candidate at Brown University who specialized in Native American Studies and explained that this quantum is very familiar with the "one-drop rule."

"Blood quantum emerged as a way to measure "Indian-ness" through a construct of race. So that over time, Indians would breed themselves out and rid the federal government of their legal duties of upholding treaty obligations."[lxxxvii]

When I spoke to Lana, I didn't understand how difficult it was to retrieve a Certificate of Blood Certification.

"Blood Quantum is a way to essentially try to show who qualifies in the Native tribes. For decades it was used to make Native tribes smaller. I am mixed race- black and Native. It has been difficult to "prove" my Native side. My mother is Native from the Lakota tribe, and my father is Black. It's been tough to get my Blood Card, because of my mixed heritage. I'm from Arkansas, and I have to fight for both sides, but to me, Blood Quantum is a movement to stop Native cultures from thriving. And to wipe out the Native culture."

Blood is to show how race is a social construct. Still, the most important thing to understand is that American Indians not only have the history of the blood quantum, but they also have legal status, unlike any other racial group. Native Americans are not technically a minority group, but they are members of an independent tribal government. Author to *the Color of Wealth*, Barbara Robles explains that the federal government has determined the rights of Indian tribes and tribal governments so that they can have tribal citizenship as a priority over American citizenship.[lxxxviii] Race and Relations within the Native American tribes create a foundation of redlining. This redlining was a pillar of discrimination between tribes, and it is a problem that tribes deal with today. Well, many of the practices that we've seen have Native Americans are very similar to redlining practices in the United States. Understanding history is critical to understand the future.

Chapter 12

Native American Women's Money Story

For the first time in history, Native American women elected to U.S. Congress: Rep. Sharice Davids of Kansas Rep. Deb Haaland, the first two Native American women to be elected to the Congress of the United States. This push is a glimmer of hope, and it's something that we should celebrate; Native American women are representing Native American Issues.

Today, Native American women in the U.S. only make, on average, 57 cents for every dollar a white American man makes. According to the American Association of University Women, the gap is particularly bad in some states, such as California, where the difference between Native American women's and non-Hispanic men's yearly wages add up to $34,833, or a whopping $1,395,320 over a lifetime.[lxxxix]

Aiyana's Story

"When I first moved to Oklahoma from California, I wanted to be around my tribe. I tried to Native culture more accessible. I'm Choctaw, and most of my family members live in Oklahoma after Trail of Tears. In high school, I started using Twitter and getting connected to my Native roots. I started getting involved in activism because I realized that many Native don't have access to traditional jobs. With the help of Twitter, I realized that I had a deep connection to Native culture, so I decided to move to be closer to my family.

Living in Oklahoma is heaven and hell. And I learned about activism more, but it's hell because I'm learning about the bad parts of my culture. I love my lifestyle, but I had no idea that some of my family members were drug users. And what upset me the most is I learned that my great grandfather forced my great-grandma to marry and he kidnapped her and forced her to move to California without her permission. That's how my family made it to California. The more I attend Native activism, I get excited, but at the same time, I feel like I'm wasting my money on living in a place where I'm learning the truth."

Aiyana's great grandmother's story of kidnap is a familiar story for Native American Women In 2016, alone, there were 5,712 cases of Native women missing, according to the National Crime Information Center.[xc] Unfortunately, only 116 were logged by the U.S. Department of Justice's federal missing person's database, according to the National Crime Information Center. [xci]

The Current Health of Native American Women

A large number of Native American women are enduring Human Rights violations. According to American Progress, Native American women are 3.5 times more likely than any other racial group to be sexually assaulted.

84 % Of indigenous women have physical, psychological, sexual violence in their lifetime, according to the National Institute of Justice.[xcii]

Who is in charge of assault is tricky because of the Native certification. A recent report by the University of Delaware and North Carolina found that "white and other non-Native American people commit more than two-thirds of sexual assaults against indigenous women."[xciii] The dilemma of jurisdiction is because non-Native men who assault women cannot be arrested by tribes or state court but only through federal court.[xciv] When I interviewed Lana and Aiyana, both mentioned that they had experienced sexual trauma during their childhood.

The mental health of Native American women because of the disenfranchisement through Historical Trauma. The UC Davis research project community Native American leader explained the current state of mental health.[xcv][xcvi]

"I am dealing with people who have been (disenfranchised) and their mental illness originates in the system around them, the environment, the surrounding historical trauma. They are not crazy; they are people responding to trauma in their life."

How does this play into Native American Women's Money Story?

When mothers are disappearing, and young women are taking advantage, it creates a lot of trauma. Although we haven't quantified the numbers behind the injury, it's pretty evident that injury can affect someone's ability to work on money.

What we know now is that many women are returning to their matriarchal roots, which is very telling after all the trauma—folks_like Amber Crotty, a lawmaker for the Navajo Nation.[xcvii] In 2019, Crotty spoke to the Department of Justice to get funding for developing laws and fix the missing person database.

Holding personal interviews for Native American women was a difficult thing to do. Even when I got in touch with someone who was Native American and in finance, they did not want to disclose their story, and that I respect. I am so grateful for the two women that decided to spend time with me. I hope that this picture sheds light for many and makes us realize that there's so much happening in our backyards that we're unaware of.

Chapter 13
Latinx Historical Money Story

Shauna's Story

A successful Mexican-American businesswoman and I sat down for virtual coffee one evening to talk about her money story. This beautiful reddish brown-skinned woman had achieved the unimaginable and finished college in California as a first-generation college student. Shauna paid off all her student loan bills in cash because she did not have the opportunity to retrieve financial aid because of her parent's status being undocumented. So, that meant she had to work multiple jobs and take care of everything. When I spoke to Shauna about her money story, Pandora's box was open, and she began to heal.

"So, I didn't know that a considerable part of my trauma happened, and it affected my childhood. And unfortunately, it wasn't a one-time thing. It was something that I had to suffer for many years. When my family came to the United States at the time, I was undocumented. For me, that meant not telling people a lot of things because there was always that fear that someone is still going to find out about me, and I would be deported

and taken away. When I was young, my mother gave birth to another child, and at that time, my newly born sibling was sick. The whole family was in and out of the hospital for out of my siblings. There was always out of money because my dad and mom had to pay for hospital bills.

There was always money scarcity; it still up (childhood me) had to figure out how to get the money. Because money was always a problem, my parents were always bickering back and forth about money. Being the oldest, my mom depended on me to be the right-hand person. That meant going to ask for money. I would have to perform for the money. And I've never said this out loud. Not even to my therapist. I would have to have a trade-off.

My father was involved with the Mexican Mafia and had money. So, whenever my mother needed money for my sibling or to pay bills, she would ask him for money. She was also 16 years old when she had me and with a 5th-grade education. She depended on me as the oldest child.

So, the abuse started. The damage began when I was very young, and it went for a decade, it was sexual abuse. There was sexual abuse from my dad. It was a transaction, and I would get the money, and I would have to perform. The molestations happened until I was 12 or 13.

I don't want to have any more secrets I don't want to hide. It's time for me to heal so that I can help others."

For Shauna, we must acknowledge that power, gender roles, and scarcity from her parents created her Adverse Childhood Experience. To understand Shauna's story and Latinx immigration, one must follow it through the lens of your grandma.

History creates the same set of patterns. Patterns are safe, and they help us to understand the world. Our money story with Latinx identity starts in 1930, around the same time your grandma or great-grandma was born. That was the wrong time for everyone because no one had the funds to support themselves through the Great Depression. When big ol' GD took place, everybody went into their own seven stages of Grief: Shock, Denial, Anger, Bargaining, Depression, Testing, and Acceptance. And the eighth stage that no one speaks about is hysteria.

Hysteria will make you think that the world is flat and standing outside overnight for a *Tickle Me Elmo* is logical. Around the time your grandmother was conceived, hysteria took over the radio like an influencer on your Instagram feed. Hysteria was the unknown gospel of xenophobia and eugenics.

Xenophobia was all the craze in the 1920s-1930s. Many people longed for a purer America. There were political talks of who deserved to be here. As we know, this was the time of the Great Depression. The Great Depression stirred a significant push for Mexican American Immigrants in 1929.

President Hoover agreed to the first mass deportation of Mexican Americans by the name of "Mexican repatriation." The first round of the repatriation raid in Los Angeles rounded people up and asked them for their papers, and if the Mexican Americans didn't take them with them, (even if they were otherwise legally in the US) they were sent on a train.

Deportation occurred even if they had citizenship papers; around sixty percent were American citizens. Many Mexican American women and children were without family members. [xcviii] Family stability is often necessary to build money. When times get rough, blame the Mexicans.

The other problematic theme was that everyone assumed that anyone who spoke Spanish was from Mexico. There are twenty-one Spanish speaking countries in Latin American filled with diverse cultural backgrounds. But that didn't matter; Americans felt that Latino/Latinx culture needed to go back so that more jobs would be for US citizens. The national rhetoric became:

"Whether they were American citizens, or whether they were Mexican nationals, in the American mind — that is, in the mind of government officials, in the mind of industry leaders — they're all Mexicans. So, ship them home. "[xcix]

Robbed of tears and leaving a culture vulnerable, the Mexican Repatriation Act opened a wound of distrust. The money story of hysteria proceeded to our next form of Hysteria: Operation Wetback.

Operation Wetback

"Wetbacks were seeping across the border at a record-breaking rate- two a minute, day and night. Like ants said Chief Patrol Inspector Ed Parker. They're Swarming over like ants. "[c]

- Time Magazine, 1953

Operation Wetback was a swarm of opinions and attitudes. During his presidency, President Dwight Eisenhower was a well-respected man and celebrated for his military leadership during WW2. His judgment influenced the masses, and during his presidency, the state of hysteria became a dark wave of American stream of consciousness.

It didn't just hit white people; every ethnic group was affected. The US hysteria undertook even Latinos US citizens. Author David Gutierrez, in his book *Walls and Mirrors*, writes that the early 1950s Mexican Americans had issues with Mexican immigrants. According to Gutierrez, Latino organizations like the League of United Latin American Citizens and the American GI. Forum wanted strict immigration because of past circumstances; many of these organizations supported the strict immigration policies the US government instituted.

Many Latino American Organizations changed their minds about strict immigration rules, but by that time, the harsh deportation rhetoric was still in progress. Keep in mind that this second wave of deportation was probably around when your mom or dad was born. The economic divide not only created a low-key group think of American society but in the end, it fueled our current political climate.

In 1955, Eisenhower approved Operation Wetback, and tens of thousands of immigrants were shoved onto buses, boats, and planes forced to move to Mexico.[ci] What made it enjoyable was that OW didn't have to use troops because, with the propaganda, the Mexican American legal and undocumented deported. It's estimated that 1.3 million experienced deportations. Through the use of radio and television, the argument claimed that "illegal" immigration was undermining wages.[cii]

For the Latinx community, federal laws that have consistently redefined the problem of immigration in America. For the past 100 years, the Latin/Hispanic American community has been a subject of constant deportation laws, and the threat of mass deportation (even for otherwise legal immigrants) has economically affected three generations.

What does this have to do with our money story?

When we look at all the manipulations of pop culture, every time mass deportation occurred was because it interfered with economic development. It's sad to say, but I've heard many of my black family members call Latinx wetbacks, and I've been in conversations where a white person has spoken about Mexicans raping their children. And sadly, this was when I was in high school, and I used to be concerned about illegal immigrants because we were all programmed to have a particular view about an entire culture.

CHAPTER 14

LATINX WOMEN'S MONEY STORIES

Latinx women are making huge strides. Between 2003 to 2013 they've raised their representation by 30 percent in receiving professional degrees. [ciii] Latinx women are healthy breadwinners in their households. According to The White House Initiative on Educational Excellence for Hispanics, it's projected that by "2060, Latinx will form nearly a third of the female population of the nation."[civ] With so much growth, we have to address the silent killer of growth and success and talk about the dilemma in Latinx's money story.

Latina women have the worst wage gap than any female ethnic group. On average, Latina women get paid 53 cents for every dollar that white man makes. This gap hurts families and contributes to a cycle of poverty. What's even more upsetting is that — thanks to the prolonged closing of the wage gap — It is projected that Latina women will not experience true pay equality until the year 2233.[cv]

The median income for Latinx communities is around $46,882 annually compared to White families, who earned a median income of $61,200. In America, the

Latinx poverty rate has hovered approximately 20% the past 40 years, according to Prosperity Now. In the past 80 years, we've created a silent beast of extreme discrimination between a group of Latinx women, and it has a lot to do with the constant wave of deportation.[cvi]

When I interviewed Lucia, a media project manager in San Diego, we talked about her experience as a Latina woman in a white-dominated field.

"When I found out that everyone in my position was getting paid higher than me, I tried to figure out how to get paid, but I couldn't talk to my family about it because I was doing much better than everyone else. My mother worked as a maid; I felt like I was complaining."

For Lucia, she wondered about other people's pay for the first time in her career. For Lucia, taught to be happy for her situation, but not speak up for compensation. She fought to get a raise, and eventually pressured her job. But Lucia was not having pay equity conversations because of her family; she had made it. Unfortunately, making it doesn't always represent stability. Even when Lucia was a citizen, it took her years in the workforce to fight for equal pay.

Mental Health in the Latinx Women's Community

"Calladita se ve más bonita." Quiet looks prettier

Gender discrimination occurs in many forms, but, culturally, Latinx women have to silence their emotions and appear "pretty" In a recent Jacqueline Priego, 34, Writer/Director/Actress, PinkSlipped Web Series, talks about the views of women in Latinx communities. She says that many women believe that it's essential to be quiet and look prettier than having opinions.

"I wish I would have known that 'quietly get your work done' and 'stay out of trouble' — the two most common albeit well-intentioned pieces of advice given to first-generation Latinxs entering the world of the 9-5 — would lead to many years of discontent."[cvii]

She is correct in saying that not only are there policies in place that can deport people, but also the cultural influence is active within the Latinx community.

This silence is taking forms in different ways particularly with Latinx adolescents. Latina adolescents have the highest rate of attempted suicide. According to the Centers for Disease Control and Prevention's 2017 US survey, 10.5% of Latina adolescents aged between 10–24 have attempted suicide in the past year, compared to 7.3% of a white female, 5.8% of Latino, and 4.6% white male teens.[cviii]

Latinx therapy is turning into an epidemic, but suicide and money are incredibly taboo topics in their community. If we don't start talking about these issues, there will be more women in a huge bind. There are women like Adriana Alejandre, LMFT founder of Latinx Therapy who is taking the stigma out of therapy. The lack of dialogue and understanding of how money and cultural effects mental health only exacerbates issues surrounding mental health for young Latinas.

A culture that is rich and vibrant has a lot of money healing and wounds that need to be solved. The taboo topics often have to deal with family dynamics. These family dynamics profoundly affect equal pay, and it would be an injustice not to acknowledge the problems that are occurring.

Colorism- Commission fee

Colorism is alive and well in the Latina historical money story. The focus on who is Latina is always a topic of discussion. When many people look at the telenovelas, it's often the lighter-skinned Latina that is at the forefront. The truth is, depending on what side of the shadow you are, it could create a different money dynamic growing up.

When I spoke to Alejandra, a successful woman in the filming industry, Alejandra was very proud of her heritage and her family upbringing. When we dove into her money story, she saw both sides of the coin that her father, who was of a darker complex and had to hustle, is way into a good life, and his mother, who was white-passing had a very different upbringing. When we had the conversation of colorism, she explained to me that her white-Hispanic side of the family paid what is known as a finder's fee.

"A finder's fee was anytime someone came into town, and someone was asking to pick your brain; you would pay them in some way, shape, or form. My white-passing side of the family would consistently pay each other forward, and that was something I learned that White families would do as well. When my mother was younger, she would spend the finder's fee, but now she had completely flipped the switch and felt that you could not mix money with family because when she interacted with money with my dad's side, they didn't pay it forward."

The money story around colorism is complex. And the brevity of this book is condensed to a finder's fee. The discussion around colorism has a significant role in the narrative of the Latinx US money story. Not only who is receiving financial access in the country, but how Latinx women are viewed.

Between gender dynamics, colorism, and deportation, all of these concepts of cultural identity are under a microscope. The conversation around worthiness and self-worth is a discussion worth sharing. American Culture has neglected a large portion of the United States, forgetting that by 2050 the projected demographic of Latinx living in the US will be 29%, according to Pew Research Center.[cix] Our conversations around Latinx culture must change to meet the needs of future generations.

Chapter 15
Now What

"All literature is political." - LeVar Burton

When I was in 8th grade, my social studies teacher, Mr. Malitano, made us all watch *Roots, The Miniseries*. What a great time it was, to go back and forth to whether Hector likes you or not. To get boobs and musk under your arms and then the icing on the cake, my white teacher said we had to watch the entire *Roots* series. Yikes!

As a 14-year-old, I couldn't find the right feelings. Did I hate white people? Why would they do this? Was something wrong with my black skin?

Meanwhile, Jessica P. blond hair blue-eyed is in disbelief that her face turned red with embarrassment. It was probably Jessica's first time seeing a slave trade boat. Did I want to tell her off? I wanted to say that her people suck. Yes, I did. But that wasn't going to help Jessica. It might have been cathartic for me, but it wouldn't have solved the problem

You might have read this first portion of the book and felt the same way I did when I was in 8th grade— confused, angry, and unsure what move to make next. You have every right to feel that way. The financial system through racial discrimination is problematic. I also understand that you might want to put this book down because it is a lot to take in. That is entirely understandable.

We must acknowledge that we all have financial PTSD. We look at the past problems, dwell on them, or put the issue out of sight and ignore the challenge. But if we don't talk about the past, this can lead to feelings of shame and guilt with not being good enough with money.

Overall Patterns of WOC

The hardest part of writing this book is portraying the real truth behind money and mental health. I had to include some trauma to inform you how our mind affects the way we earn money. But I also wanted to let you know that all of the 40 women were successful in their own right. Around 75% of them had a business. A large portion of them were the sole breadwinners in their families. Like I mentioned earlier, many of them were college-educated, but it was my job to find the thing that keeps them up at night.

There are a few patterns that I wanted to mention that all of the women have collectively experienced. Throughout every conversation, there was a strong sense of feeling that they work so hard, but it will never be enough. All the women portrayed these feelings in different ways. For some, it was the feeling of never being enough for their family. For some scarcity played out in, I'll never be enough at work or in their environment. Regardless of how badass the individual was, scarcity was also the fuel to their fire and the reason for their success.

All strived to help themselves and help others figure out their families' money story. Every single woman had a family that they were worried about, and many of them were the "success story" in their families. All of these women are superwomen. But when do superwomen ever get the chance to take off their capes and relax? Lastly, everyone that I interviewed was giving back and helping their community in some capacity. Through podcasts or businesses, these women all helped their culture discover their truths and realities in addition to working.

Shauna's Story

I wanted to wrap up with Shauna's story from the Latinx women's chapter because her story was the most complicated and complex story that I had to listen to. During our interview, I remember shutting the camera off and sobbing uncontrollably. I want to acknowledge that I was the first person that she told her story to. What faith she had in me. Shauna was balling, making it with a six-figure business and was the breadwinner of her family, but had a lot of pain.

I want to note that after Shauna told her truth to me, a year later, she was telling people her story on social media and talking to her therapist about it. We even had additional phone calls about how to save more money and invest. We researched different financial BFFs that wouldn't shame her but acknowledge her past. We found books from financial therapists to help her see how money, sex, and drugs from her father's abuse affected her money decisions.

Like Shauna, the goal for all of us is to look at your historical background and craft a financial plan that personalizes your health, wealth, relationships, and family. In the next portion of the book, we're going to look at our holistic view of your money.

PART TWO

HOLISTIC GUIDE TO FINANCIAL WELLNESS

Chapter 16
Financial Wellness 101

What does it mean to be financially well?

Have you ever had a calm conversation with your friend or family and said, "I don't think I'm well with my money, can you help me?" Chances are you haven't had "The talk" unless you were in a crisis or are planning for a significant life change like marriage or moving. It's because many of us are not comfortable in talking about our money to the ones we love. But the truth is that money is a holistic part of our lives and without it, we are unable to live. Which is why we must see money as a key part of our lives. We can figure out how money affects our lives and this method is called Financial Wellness.

Financial Wellness is a flashy buzz word that is often misused and somewhat confusing. It makes sense because Financial Wellness hasn't been well researched or tested. Fortunately, we have done historical work to look at how the past has affected our money story. Now, it's up to us to personalize our past and create a holistic view of our money story. So, if we were to create a term for financial wellness it would be:

Financial Wellness is the act of learning about how your personality, environment, and experiences affect your money habits which will lead to financial stability. Financial Wellness is the act of understanding your financial cycle.

It's important to identify that Financial Wellness is cyclical and not linear. The US Department of Health and SAMHSA created a holistic path that was drafted for wellness. According to SAMHSA, if we were to look through the lens of the wellness eight pillars, we could figure out how financial wellness can help us with our Money Story.[cx] The eight wellness pillars are:

1. Physical

2. Nutritional

3. Emotional

4. Social

5. Spiritual

6. Intellectual

7. Financial

8. Environmental.

If we want to be well, we ALL have to unpeel layers of our financial well-being by looking at the eight pillars of wellness. Every person's money story is different and unique, which is why we need to have a genuinely holistic approach to money. This is the path to becoming financially well. As we begin to look at each of these eight pillars, we will ask ourselves how each one affects our money story.

Chapter 17

Physical Pillar- Get Some Sleep!

"It's also our collective delusion that overwork and burnout are the prices we must pay in order to succeed."
- Arianna Huffington

"Get into a state of rest whenever you can. You will have to be subversive and inventive sometimes. You are a resistor. Rest."
- The Nap Ministry

Everything happens in the physical. Physical wellness consists of physical activity, nutrition, and sleep.[cxi] There are millions of books that talk about how we present ourselves, communicate, eat, and, of course, exercise, but there are only a few books that highlight the joy of sleeping. Today, we're going to uncover how sleep affects our money stories and how it affects decision making.

We've all started a trend of competitive sleep deprivation.[cxii]I can remember talking to a chipper girl in one of my financial wellness workshops. During our session, she explained to the group that the sleep doctor told her that she was one of those small percentages of people that thrive after only having five hours of sleep. I was so impressed by her personal data that I started researching it. I kept thinking to myself maybe I should sleep less.

As I was researching heavily the benefits of sleeping less, I noticed a large flaw in the research. As it turns out, the ability to sleep for five to six hours was only proven by one scientific study conducted by the University of San Diego in 2010 and reported that "women who slept between 5.0 and 6.5 hours each night were likely to live longer than those who slept more or less." This study took the world by storm. [cxiii]

Bloggers and journalists were raving about it and the ideas were taken as truth. What was interesting was that the study said that people could "survive" between 5.0 and 6.5. There are many other studies from Oxford, Cambridge, and Harvard have found that "a lack of sleep can wreck your body clock and increase the risk of severe health problems, including cancer, heart disease, type-2 diabetes, and obesity." The benefits of sleeping less still haven't been retested as the best option, and the rhetoric is damaging.

On a historical level, Thomas Edison was the OG of sleep deprivation. Edison told Scientific American that he only needed four hours a day and forced employees to follow this rule. Not only was a lack of sleep praised within the business world, but many self-help books authors like Dale Carnegie praised this Edison for sleep deprivation.

Sleep deprivation has now become the badge of honor in business and leadership. The more senior you are at work, the less sleep you get. Professionals get an average of six hours or less[cxiv]The problem is that seventy-two percent of managers say that they have trouble focusing due to lack of sleep This contribution is from taking their work home, they're less productive at work.[cxv] They end up working at the office and can become tired, but then they end up working at home and become even more tired.

On an economical level, there is a huge loss of money when we don't sleep. It is said that time is our most valuable asset in life. We are all fighting for time and it is through the allocation of work, play, and sleep, a large chunk of us chooses work or play. The Center for Disease Control and Prevention has declared the United States insufficient sleep as a national 'public health' problem.[cxvi] The OECD collected data from all over the world to discover five countries: Canada, the US, UK, Germany, and Japan have a large economic cost of insufficient sleep.[cxvii] From these five countries, it has been stated by the OECD has lost up to 3% of the GDP costing the countries billions of dollars.[cxviii]

How many times have you powered through a workday only to find yourself being too tired to cook, so you purchase takeout? How many of you pulled an all-nighter thinking that you do well under pressure? How many of you brag about working hard with a lack of sleep (I'm guilty of this)? How many of you go online shopping when you should be sleeping?

Questions to ask yourself:	Yes	No
Do you get more than six hours of sleep a night?		
Do you "thrive" off five hours of sleep? Have you gone to a sleep specialist?		
Is there something that is keeping you up at night?		
Do you go (shopping, eating out, etc) when you are tired?		
Do you believe that procrastination is a part of your execution process?		

Chapter 18
Environmental Pillar–Safe Space

Being aware of your physical environment can dramatically change what you do and how you live. Your environment, both your social and natural surroundings, can greatly impact how you feel about your life as a whole. Our environment is the most critical aspect because it's what keeps us grounded. Even if you consider yourself an explorer, and live in multiple countries or cities, it's essential to think about the place you call home.

We all have to grapple with it because if we're primarily influenced by our physical space, it's imperative to go beyond just cleaning up our home or purchasing a self-help book. Unstable environments can affect our spending.

Philadelphia

(P.S. To all my Philadelphians, read the whole thing before you try to "clap" back...)

For most of my adult life, I was a nomad. I had the privilege, plus the frugality, to live in different spaces, southern, tropical, city, rural, etc. The question of how my money is reflecting my environment was utterly foreign to me until I entered my thirties.

When I moved to Philadelphia, all of my ideas went out of the door.

The ethos of the birthplace of America is filled with a complicated history but is infused with hustle. In all honesty, the hero's journey is significant to Philadelphians, which is why there is a Rocky Statue where millions of tourists travel to run the Rocky Steps. It took me a while to figure out what the deal was because I never lived in a place where a football game could dramatically affect people's moods.

It took me three years to discover this but living in Philadelphia stressed me out because I was a recovering Type-A/hustler. Literally everyone I knew had a side hustle. I always felt that I had to be doing more and I started overworking like crazy. I spent way more for an apartment, even though Philadelphia is really inexpensive for rent. I panicked, I over hustled and overworked more than I ever had. I didn't know that Philadelphia was ranked as one of the unhappiest cities and also the worst place for sleep.

It took me a while to realize that I must get a little meta and embrace the people and flow instead of hustle. Since moving to Philadelphia I had to rethink what I watched, listened to, and even track my sleeping habits. No more entrepreneur videos for me. I may be working hard to accomplish goals, but I don't need to out-hustle anyone. Our environment can create strange patterns that we aren't aware of, but it's essential to recognize that it influences us.

Chapter 19

Emotional Pillar-Your ACE Score

Our emotional pillar affects every aspect of our lives, how we interact with ourselves and our jobs. But not only do we manage our emotions, but we also manage others too! We're going to look at the present and past feelings to better understand our future.

Present: How do you Manage your Mood?

All we have is the present. The trickiest question to ask is, why are we looking at the past and present to dictate our futures? Because our brains are always focusing on making habits from the past, we lose track of what's present. Also, we live in a world where most of us are future-oriented. So, we're going to complete an activity to find out where we stand with our emotions. I use this mood journal as a daily activity courtesy of *Healthline*.[cxix] You can use this activity daily.

What emotions are you currently feeling right now?

What caused this emotion?

Behaviors or actions this emotion caused me to take

Is this emotion appropriate to the situation?

Is this situation distress to be tolerated or a problem to solve? And how?

Past

 In chapter 7, we talked about the Adverse Childhood Experience (ACE). Your ACE Score is a metric that can help you understand some of your mental health problems. Based on your past, you can learn a lot about current struggles. My ACE score of 2 helped me uncover that I had an anxious attachment style. This anxiousness affected my health and emotions in turn. It also made me spiral entirely out of balance whenever I lost money.

It is important to note that ACE Scores don't take into account the positive factors of your life. ACE scores cannot calculate how discrimination, resilience, or your physical environment have played a role. And ACE scores do not dictate your entire emotional well-being, but it does help you see what risks there are.

You're going to take the ACE to see where you are. If you are uncomfortable with this, skip it. If you want to complete this activity with a mental health specialist, you may do that as well. I know you've overcome a lot of adversities to get where you are, but like you, I didn't see how the past affected my future.

Questions to ask yourself: For each "yes" answer, add 1. The total number at the end is your cumulative number of ACEs. Before your 18th birthday	Yes	No
Did a parent or other adult in the household often or very often... Swear at you, insult you, put you down, or humiliate you? Or Act in a way that made you afraid that you might be physically hurt?		
Did a parent or other adult in the household often or very often... Push, grab, slap, or throw something at you? Or ever struck you that you had marks or were injured?		
Did a household member go to prison?		
Was a household member depressed or mentally ill, or did a household member attempt suicide?		
Did an adult or person at least 5 years older than you ever... Touch or fondle you or have you sexually touch their body? or Attempt or have oral, anal, or vaginal intercourse with you?		
Did you live with anyone who was a problem drinker or alcoholic, or who used street drugs?		
Are your parents separated or divorced?		

Did you often or very often feel that ... No one in your family loved you or thought you were important or special? or Your family didn't look out for each other, feel close to each other, or support each other?		
Did you often or very often feel that ... You didn't have enough to eat, had to wear dirty clothes, and had no one to protect you?		

Source: Harvard Center for Childhood Development, NPR, ACEsTooHigh.com. This ACEs Quiz is a variation on the questions asked in the original ACE study conducted by CDC researchers.[cxx]

Your emotions have a large portion with how you look at your money story. As we mentioned in previous chapters, there have been a lot of policies that have been put in place to disenfranchise Women of Color. Understanding how your past can determine your future has a long history. Your emotional well-being has so many layers to it and can affect your money story on many levels. While on paper, this is easier said than done, the path toward emotional well-being requires constant attention. We must understand that our emotions have a strong correlation to how we spend our money.

How does the emotional aspect affect your money story?

How does my ACE score affect how I feel about my money story?

Have you sought out other services to address your past

Chapter 20
Social Pillar–Your Personal
Relationship

How do we interact within the global world? The Social Pillar takes human interaction on a different scope because it deals with our expectations of the world. Who we interact with successfully can have an effect on how we create a network of friends and family.[cxxi] But first, we must uncover what our expectations and demands are.

Most behavior patterns and social interactions derive from our families. Who we interact with growing up, and what the social norms were from your childhood. Where we stand, many of us live very close to the birthplace that we grew up in. In fact, a typical American lives 18 miles away from their mom, according to the Health and Retirement Study.[cxxii] Except for college or military, around 37% have never left their hometown, and 57% of people never left their home state.[cxxiii] For most of us, how we interact is similar to when we were children because it's all we know. How do my social interactions affect my relationship with money?

If your family relationships are complicated and super interconnected, you have to unpack them. Oftentimes, your relationship can be heavily influenced by your family's money story. If your family doesn't talk about money with their friends, you're likely to do the same. If your parents spend below their means, you're likely to follow in their footsteps. It is essential to think about how you interact with your family on a social level.

Friendships

Everything we do with our friend's costs money. From happy hours to birthday parties, friendships take a bulk of our budget. We typically don't talk about money, but we spend it because it has a lot of significance to our associations. According to Anna Sale, podcaster of Death, Sex and Money, "money can feel like a measure of self-worth and a way to define ourselves." Most friends support us emotionally, but what happens if they don't?

We typically fall into a pattern where we hang out with people because they attended the same school as us, or we met them at work. Our social media is very homogenous and niched. We like who we like, and we hate who we hate. Psychologist, Meg Jay talks about this in her book, The Defining Decade that urban tribes help us survive, but not always thrive. Jay encourages people to step out of their comfort zone and learn about new things and meet new people. It's hard not to fall into a tribe; the most important thing to remember is how does my urban tribe affect my money story?

When we think about our social pillar it's essential to separate ourselves from our social spaces and ask following the question:

Is what I'm doing with my money a reflection of my family's situation or of my most authentic self?

Is what I'm doing with my money a reflection of my friend's situation or of my most authentic self?

How do my social interactions affect my relationship with money?

Chapter 21
Intellectual Pillar–How do You spend your time?

How do you spend your mental time?

Our minds need constant stimulation, but the question is what is the best way to stimulate our intellectual wellness? In the information age it's difficult to get into the flow of creativity, without being a distraction. Not finding what you're passionate about can block your creativity and, in the long run, your learning growth.

Intellectual wellness is the act of participating in cultural, creative, and community activities.[cxxiv] When we engage in intellectual wellness, we are able to expand our skills which creates value in lifelong learning. The reason why a lot of us are stuck with intellectual wellness is that we still look at it as one dimensional. Read a book, go to school.

In this time, we have the opportunity to fuel ourselves with all different facets of learning. This is a portion of our intellect. This is where we have to cut out the crap and find our passion. Our passion is the act of getting lost in time and engaging in a task that is strenuous enough that our mind, body, and spirit is activated. As woo as that sounds, we need to find ways to activate our minds in unique ways.

We need to spend time learning and being creative, but it seems like there is never enough time. It can take at least thirty minutes to focus on something without distractions. We also feel like we have to create routines to be creative and have to calendar it out.

The rise of the knowledge economy has helped us, but it has also made us stifle our creativity. So, it is important to ask, am I using my brain to stimulate my creativity, or am I just following the status quo?

Question Within the last year I have....	Yes	No
Take a course or workshop		
Learn (or perfect) a foreign language?		
Seek out people who challenge you intellectually		
Read or listen to audiobooks		

Chapter 22

Spiritual Pillar - The Feeling of AWE

Who is drinking the Kool-aid?

Spirituality is a messy topic. The fluidity of spirituality is always strange, so many of us don't think about how it affects our money stories. In this chapter, we'll talk about the emotional state of being in awe.

The Feeling of AWE

There is something about the feeling of being in sync with an act that feels greater than yourself. Like when you reach the top of climbing a mountain. Your feet look below, and you see the mountaintop and feel powerful and powerless at the same time. Or when you participate in religious connectedness. You are in a group of people that all believe in the same thing as you. For some of us, we have a complete out of body experience. All of these experiences can bring us to a sense of awe.

Awe is the feeling of self-diminishment (to make it smaller or less) or and the ability to be connected with other people.[cxxv] Professor of Psychology, Dacher Keltner, explains that when we feel as if we are in awe, we put ourselves in a self-transcendent state where we focus less on ourselves and feel more like a larger whole.[cxxvi] The positive aspects of AWE provide positive physical experience through emotions. Experiences of awe can give physiological effects through goosebumps.[cxxvii]

In the workplace, many people can create their sense of awe through company culture. We spend a third of our lives working. As our world becomes overloaded with information, we desire to find more niche ways of being connected. Younger generations look for jobs that provide a purpose in their lives. This is why companies with a greater work culture are some of the fastest-growing ones.

I am a culture driven employee. Every job I've had required me to learn about the culture and values first. This can be a positive or negative thing, but for me, I had to realize that I am a Kool-aid drinker of company culture, and it dramatically affected my money story. I would work for a company and not question pay or think about my financial future because I had to work for the company. *How do you experience awe?*

Spirituality

Growing up, I was in the church at least three times a week. My family grew up in the South, so there was a strong sense of Southern Baptist roots. Historically, the church is considered a social hub in African American Culture. Post-Civil War, the church played a crucial role in strengthening African American Communities, and it created leverage for the Civil Rights Movement.[cxxviii] This is why roughly eight out of ten African Americans self-identify as Christian, according to the Pew Research Center.

Most of my experiences of awe were founded by religion. The older I get, the more appreciative of Christianity I am, but I have also realized that a lot of forms of spirituality have positive and negatives. On the positive side, it creates connectedness. It is one of the few times that I *genuinely feel* connected to Black Culture.

On the negative side, I learned that much of my money conversation as a child was solely on tithing to a church. As a child, I started working every job that I could. I helped out at the children's church. I participated in a praise dance at my school. I followed the rules, and I tried hard not to disobey, although I did get into trouble from time to time.

One of the first disagreements with the church was money. I used to get angry around the minister asking for money. I would look around at my small church and ask how could we spend ten minutes on paying tithes when we can't pay ourselves? There used to be people that had no money and couldn't pay their bills but would give ten percent of their income in the hopes of being blessed. I used to ask people about it, but I never received an actual answer.

There was a specific time during every church service, right after praise and worship, when people would take at least 15 minutes to talk about the importance of tithing. Singing is one of the few times where we feel super connected to a sense of connectedness. When we are experiencing awe or flow, our rational brain is out the window. It is when we experience awe. They would quote several bible verses.

Leviticus 27:30-34

And a tenth part of the herd and of the flock, whatever goes under the rod of the valuer, will be holy to the Lord.

Numbers 18:26

Say to the Levites, When you take from the children of Israel the tenth which I have given to you from them as your heritage, the tenth part of that tenth is to be offered as an offering lifted up before the Lord.

Encouraging people to tithe isn't the problem, it's how the tithing takes place right after experiencing the feeling of AWE. By placing a percentage, it is looking at things for face value. It can evoke shame. It took me a while to understand how connected I thought my prosperity was to spirituality.

Chapter 23

Nutritional Pillar – Seeking Relief through Food

Do you know that the average annual budget groceries and going out is $7,700?[cxxix] Food is fuel; it also provides social experiences. It changes and fluctuates depending on what is happening within your life. In many ways, your nutrition can determine how you spend your money. When you are stressed or feeling yourself, knowing how to treat your food based on your needs, not anyone else can influence your money story.

Most of the nutritional beliefs we get are old ideas. Do you remember when you were a kid, and your school explained the food pyramid to you? Some of our first conversations were at school. For decades, the U.S. Department of Agriculture explained to us children that the most critical food we should eat is 6-11 servings of bread, cereal, etc. Everything else, including fruits and vegetables. Now, as adults, many of us, our beliefs, are from inaccurate facts.

Many of us still have the notion that we should be strict with eating nutrition. Some of us get overwhelmed by food and ignore it completely. Especially when we are in crisis or focused on our careers, we create black and white rules for being healthy. We have to be Keto; it's time for Paleo. Let's go on a diet. For the purpose of this book, we're going to take a deep dive into eating.

What are your eating habits?

Earlier in the book, I talked about how my dad created a habit of drinking *Coke*. If you recall, a feedback loop consists of a loop at the core of every pattern. Each habit has a circuit that consists of three parts: A cue, a routine, and a reward. The Cue is a signal to tell you that you should be doing something. The method is the actual act of a habit, and lastly, the reward is the feeling that one receives after performing the task. If we look at my dad's habit

Cue: Girlfriend Mom is sick

Routine: Weekly visits to the hospital

Reward: Coke; my dad felt like he belonged to a family.

Here's another example: My old stress eating habit

Cue: Have a rough day at work

Routine: Go and complain to my best friend

Reward: We drive to Shake Shack and get hamburgers with friends. We complain together and eat food together.

Now, it's your turn to do this activity:

Cue:

Routine:

Reward:

Questions to ask yourself: Within the last month I have....	Yes	No
When you are stressed, do you eat?		
Do you have plans for grocery shopping?		
Do you seek comfort food weekly?		
Do you spend more money on take-out and/or eating out than groceries?		
Do you beat yourself up for spending too much money on food?		

Chapter 24
Financial Pillar - The Basics We Forget

Everything we do costs money. Looking at the financial pillars, we recognized that we've never created the right vocabulary to really talk about financial stability. Many of us feel guilty about not being able to reach our financial potential and this, in turn, affects our mental health.

Never feeling enough with our money can lead to constant stress on our mental health. From remembering bills to keeping track of spending or finding the best deal on bills. When we have financial difficulty, it makes us more likely to "fall behind on payments or struggle to repay the credit." It becomes a vicious cycle. These feelings often lead to shame, anger, frustration.

Most people never talk about how financial difficulties affect their mental health. This is in part because, in the United States, we haven't entirely tied in our mental health and money together.

Now, on the positive side, there are government programs to ensure how to manage money like the Consumer Financial Protection Bureau (CFPB). This agency ensures that you as a consumer get help on paying late bills, talking to debt collectors, and which companies are creating. An emerging field of Financial Therapy is also taking place. A collective of therapists, financial counselors, and financial practitioners. Folks are recognizing that looking at the "combined approach informed by both therapeutic and financial competencies, **financial therapists** are equipped to help people reach their financial lives." [cxxx]As of now, the only way that we can get this in front of decision-makers is if we tap at the corporate level and say that financial difficulties are affecting our work productivity. This is the exact method that the Money and Mental Health Institute drives home. For this activity, you will ask yourself questions about your money.

Questions to Ask Yourself	Yes	No
Do you budget or have a cash flow statement?		
Do you avoid your bank account at all costs?		
Do you have a financial accountability partner?		
Did your parents teach you about money?		
Do you have retirement?		
Do you have savings?		

Don't worry, because in the next portion we're going to organize your life and make sure you get into the habit of taking care of your finances and beyond.

Part Three

YOUR 6 NO B.S. WEEK FINANCIAL WELLNESS PLAN

Chapter 25

Financial Wellness Plan

Your Financial Wellness Plan: The 6 Week Process

Week 1: Money Date 101- learn precisely how to start the habit of building your money plan.

Week 2: Your Money Story-Uncover your money story; this is where we uncover the crap and help you understand your money blocks.

Week 3: Financial Wellness Plan--Where we look at your Wellness Pillars and find out what are some strengths and areas of growth.

Week 4: The Money Plan- This is where we uncover all your money and spending.

Week 5: Week 5: Your Net Worth We look at your net worth and credit score

Week 6: Money Brain Dumps and Money Goals- Where we plan your future

The biggest hurdle that most of us have with money is figuring out what to do next. It's incredibly hard to decipher which budget or cash flow app would work for our personalities. Many of us get frustrated with the status quo and do not take action to figure out our money stories.

Most money books are still how a man sees the money game. And the strategies ignore all historical context with how women view money or create value systems. We still have this black and white view of our money. It's either you're a rational investor, or you're a crazy Gen Wii that mismanages your money and purchases avocado toast. We have to throw all of those ideas out and start a new one. Of course, we will use actionable steps that use math to help us look at our money, but we must start thinking about our cash flow as an individualized process. But there is good news, and there is bad news.

The good news is we are witnessing women build empires at a fast rate and help other women. We have organizations and books that are assisting women in creating a seat at the table. We have books by women talking about money and building it.

The bad news is that we have to be extra vigilant when handling our money. We've seen it before where large scales of women have gotten screwed over financially. The statistics are staggering about women being taken advantage of by their wealth. We have to be our lawyers, accountants, and therapists. But we don't have to do it alone. I'll be there, and others will help you too!

The bad/good news is we are going to have to be honest about our money, which means we're going to do something completely unorthodox. We have to understand our patterns. We have to understand our lotus flower experience and figure out our money story.

It is your new plan to figure out what to do with your money. In each part, I guide you to help you figure out what your money patterns and habits are. You can use all of these techniques to help you throughout your life.

The rest of the book could be a step-by-step process if you chose it to be. The more I teach these concepts to people, I recognize that building money habits and systems can take years or more to process. I typically look at all of my different aspects at different times on an annual basis. My goal was to make this process reusable in every aspect of your life.

If you would like to download the 6 week no b.s. Financial wellness in worksheet form, you can access the 35 page documents at
https://eugeniegeorge.com/financialwellnessplan.
The access code is in the back of the book.

CHAPTER 26
WEEK 1: MONEY DATES

I don't know about you, but when I first started budgeting, I thought I had to have everything "planned" out. I would read a budgeting book. Download an app. I would map on my calendar; it is the first day to rest in my new life. I would attend money seminars only to find myself BORED OUT OF MY MIND. I knew I wanted to understand my money, but it got overwhelming because I was trying to be a perfectionist.

With that, perfectionism was a significant culprit of failing to understand my money story/ I didn't know how to invest in myself, and I didn't know how to ask for help. I tried to perfect my money habits but refused to forgive myself if I made a mistake. Like the stock market, there are ebbs and flows with the market, so are our money habits. This is why we should make money dates.

Money dates are a way to create a new relationship with your money. A Money Date is an act of setting the time on your schedule weekly, monthly, and quarterly to look at your money.

The ultimate goal is to create a habit of looking at your money. Also, money dates sound better than budgeting because of the word association. We have a negative emotion around the word budget. Money Dates don't have to be one type of budgeting meeting; it can handle a variety of things. There are four money dates that you can have throughout the month.

1. Planning Dates

2. Guidance Dates

3. Inspiration Dates

4. Education Dates

Planning Dates

The ultimate goal for planning is to look at your money consistently. Planning dates are the blueprint behind your money. It helps you plan what exactly you want to do with your cash flow. You figure out what to do with your payments, bill, and paychecks. It is where you look at the overview of your money. Do you have apps to track your money? Should you get rental insurance? The planning dates are critical to set benchmarks.

A Planning Date is an act of creating short- and long-term goals in your money. Planning Dates might take longer if this is your first time figuring out your money. These dates are detail-oriented because you're trying to figure out the best outcome for your money. Some of the Planning Dates might entail the following:

1. Scheduling Money Dates

2. Organizing your money files

3. Budgeting- Creating a budget

4. Crafting a long-term money

Guidance Dates

We all have blind spots, especially when dealing with money. Guidance dates are the act of reflecting on your money habits. Scheduling time out to see what is going on in your life and what areas need improvement is essential. Do I have an old hospital bill lurking? Should I talk to a lawyer about this? Identifying blind spots is vital for asking the right person to help you.

One important thing to note is that you don't want to jump in and purchase a product or services after you have a conversation with individuals, we want you to use this to reflect, which is an integral part of self-awareness.

Some of the Guidance Dates might entail the following:

1. Writing a Money Journal prompt.

2. You are writing out your money story.

3. Going to therapy and talking about money.

4. Reading about Trauma.

Inspiration Dates

Need time to dream? Want to learn a language, but don't have the time or money? Inspiration Money Dates are those types of dates. Having creativity with your money helps you track your planning money dates. Do you need a Pinterest board of goals or aspirations, or are you a journaler, who needs to write out their deepest secrets?

Inspiration dates are the act of figuring out what you need in order to live your best life. It's essential to take time out to dream and reorganize your goals. We are all unique, and we need the inspiration to keep motivated. You can find money inspirations most unconventionally. Every quarter, my bonus kid and I take a trip to IKEA. We chat about spaces and what the potential house would look like, plus we like the Swedish meatballs.

Some of the Inspiration Dates might entail the following:

1. Pinning future travel trips on Pinterest.

2. Looking at Zillow at houses in your neighborhood.

3. Learn more about your dream job.

4. Making a Vision Board.

Searching for Money Mentors or Influencers will inspire your dates. Money mentors can help you find your tribe. Knowing who is a couple of steps ahead of you in their journey is not only vital, but it's the fuel to your financial plan. In my podcast, Money and Flow mompreneur, Kenya Moses said that motivational speaker, Lisa Nichols, influenced her to learn more about her money. In your money journey, it's essential to look at women or men that will inspire you to take action. Finding Mentors that match your archetype is critical for success.

Education Dates

Education Dates is the act of learning about money and growing your money brain. Financial Literacy is bae. Learning about cash via *YouTube* videos, books, and courses are all necessary for your growth. Financial Literacy creates positive long-term effects. When you are planning, money articles and budget bloggers will increase your knowledge and curiosity about money. Some of the Education Dates might entail the following:

1. Read books about money.

2. Learn about negotiation skills.

3. Learn more about your dream job.

4. Researching Financial Tribes.

I want you to keep in mind that just because an educator says something, does not mean it is your journey or destiny. I want to stress that even though you are embarking on educational purposes, the important thing that we want you to be aware of is that no educational/financial literacy provides all services.

Week 1 Action Items:

Step 1: Find time to meet with your money.

Find a time on your calendar for a Money Date that fits on your schedule—every week for the next three months.

Step 2: Type in your Calendar which Type Date You are having

1. Planning Dates.

2. Guidance Dates.

3. Inspiration Dates.

4. Education Dates.

Step 3: Ya done

Chapter 27
Week 2: Your Money Story

"Whenever you should doubt your self-worth, remember the lotus flower. Even though it plunges to life from beneath the mud, it does not allow the dirt that surrounds it to affect its growth or beauty."

— *Suzy Kassem, Rise and Salute the Sun: The Writings of Suzy Kassem*

You have a mission in life. Your contribution to the world is just as significant as your life purpose. To become a lotus flower, you must first understand your crap, sift through it, and create new patterns. You must put your facemask on before helping others.

Our Money Stories look at who you were in the past to determine different scenarios in the future. It's a Ghanian tradition called Sankofa. Sankofa means "to go back and get it." We are going to find our gems or knowledge that our wisdom is based on and figure out your money story.

Creating your Money Story is considered a Guidance Date because you're paying attention to your past identity and mindset. Your previous status is where we understand your money and your family's money story. If you need a professional like a therapist or financial coach, you can use these guided questions to talk with an expert. This process can take a day or years, use your judgment to tackle this.

Step 1: Write out Your Money Story

Time to grab a piece of paper, or you can even make notes in this book. There is no one right or wrong answer.

What was your first experience with money? Describe it in detail. Did you have any positive or negative feelings towards it?

What are some positive aspects of learning about your money?

How do your parents interact with money?

How do your friends interact with money?

Keep in mind there are so many different ways for reflections but getting to know who you are is always important when it comes to your money.

Step 2: Organize Your life

After your money reflection, think about what parts need to get organized a little more in your life. Do you need to start a file cabinet for your money? Are the holidays coming up? Write a running list of essential money tasks.

Step 3: Look at your calendar and see if your Money Date time fits in with your schedule

Things change, and emergencies happen. Check-in with yourself and see if the allotted time you set fits your habits.

Step 4: Celebrate that you've gone through 2 money dates.

Chapter 28
Week 3: Your Financial Wellness Pillar

Each of us has a unique identity for our money. Your goal is to see how each of the financial wellness pillars play a role within your life. It would be considered a mix of inspiration and guidance. In this portion, you will write out how you are feeling now with your current financial wellness pillar. For this exercise, you will look at all eight pillars and find one positive aspect of this pillar (Glow). And one area that you would like to see a change in (Grow).

Step 1: Complete your Financial Wellness Pillars

Physical Pillar: Your pillar includes sleep, hygiene, and physical activity. If we were to look at your physical wellness, ask yourself the following questions:

Physical Pillar Glows: What's one positive thing going on in this pillar?

Physical Pillar Grow: What's one area that you would like to see change?

Nutritional Pillar: How am I taking care of my nutrition?

Nutritional Pillar Glows: What's one positive thing going on in this pillar?

Nutritional Pillar Grow: What's one area of growth that I am working on with my nutrition?

Emotional Pillar: (mental health, relationships, etc.)

Emotional Pillar Glows: What's one positive thing going on in this pillar?

Emotional Pillar Grow: What's one area of growth?

Spiritual: The feeling of AWE, Company Culture, the practice of worship, community

Spiritual Pillar Glows: What's one positive thing going on in this pillar?

Spiritual Pillar Grow: What's one area of growth?

Social Pillar: How am I taking care of my nutrition?

Social Pillar Glows: What's one positive thing going on in this pillar?

Social Pillar Grows: What's one area of growth that I am working on with my social interactions?

Environmental Pillar: (Where you live, hangout, spaces)

Environmental Pillar Glow: What's one positive thing going on in this pillar?

Environmental Pillar Grow: What's one area of growth?

Financial Pillar: Budget, Money, etc.

Financial Pillar Glows: What's one positive thing going on in this pillar?

Financial Pillar Grow: What's one area of growth?

Keep in mind that there are so many different ways for reflections but getting to know who you are is always important with regards to your money.

Step 2: Organize Your life

After your money reflection, think about what parts need to get organized a little more in your life. Do you need to start a file cabinet for your money? Are the holidays coming up?

Write a running list of essential tasks.

Step 3: Look at your calendar and see if your Money date fits in with your schedule.

Things change and emergencies happen. Check-in with yourself and see if the allotted time you set fits your habits.

Step 4: Celebrate that you've gone through three money

dates.

Chapter 29
Week 4: The Money Plan

Can you believe we made it this far? Through this journey, we have identified why our culture, personality, and huge barriers affect our money story. Together, we have identified how our money personality and strengths play a substantial role in determining how we handle money. This week four plans of the book we will complete the following:

1. Organize Our Money Environment.

2. Look at our Bank Activity.

3. Write out our money story narrative.

How you organize your life is a direct correlation to how you hold your money. Now, I'm not talking about being super rigid with your plans and budget, but you have to ask yourself the question: Is my environment affecting the relationship I have with money?

In previous chapters, we discussed how our environment plays a massive role in our money stories. When it comes to living our best lives, we MUST get in the habit of making our money chic. We have to organize our money stories. Where we uncover all your money, this Money Date might take longer, and it might take multiple money dates.

Step 1: Organization Your Money Environment

It is essential that you organize your money environment. I have to put on my momma bear hat and tell you that you have to put in some work. You have to learn about all aspects of your money because if you don't, someone will be in ownership of it without you even knowing. When I first started out learning about money, I hated doing it, but it turned out to save me the most amount of pain.

The first step in organizing your life is purchasing a notepad and a file cabinet.

Why is that important? Because you have to coordinate all aspects of your money and budgeting and keeping it in a file cabinet is adulting. If you want to purchase a budgeting notebook or an everyday piece of paper, in addition to buying a file cabinet, that's a smart idea too!

For the people that are angry at me now, I prepared you for this during money dates one through three. I know that there are some opposing ideas because I've been there, and I'll be able to address them.

1. But I love tech, so I won't organize it via paper.

Years ago, my two favorite money bloggers, The Broke Millennial and Dominique Broadway of Finances Demystified, used to have a no week spend challenge. The no week spend challenge required some form of tech, plus writing out whether you spent or not. The valuable lesson that I learned was that when you write things down on paper, you have a clear memory of if you spent money that day or not.

The idea of tracking on paper has stuck with me, and it's a question that I get asked on a regular basis. In many of the financial wellness classes I teach, participants ask me if they can organize online. Or which one is better for budgeting, apps, or pen and paper? I always say the pen is mightier than the sword at first, but the best option is a hybrid version of tech and document. It's because when we first start out, it's figuring out your spending habits over time.

I use two methods; the bullet journal, and an excel spread via *Tiller Money*. We live in a tech society, so it's essential to monitor your money both ways, plus we are a card-driven society, so we can miss something when we write it down and our cards track everything.

2. It's not my style to write my money down.

For all my flow goers that had resistances in their heart as soon as I used my mother voice, just know that I understand your fears. I've had clients that were considered flowy and said that when we work together, they have feelings of wanting to punch me and hug me at the same time equally. So, let me put it in terms that work. You are a Badass. You must track your money to help others be badasses. When you open your heart to your money patterns, you can heal more people.

Step 2: Organize your file cabinet.

For you to locate your money patterns, you must direct them in the right way. In the most basic terms, you have to label your file cabinets. In the past year of training, I've noticed that people tag their money in a variety of ways. Organize your life in a way that works for you.

Direct

- *Transportation*
- *Rent*
- *Electricity*
- *Insurance*
- *Investments*
- *Student Loans*

Lifestyle Categories

- *Health*
- *Wealth*
- *Relationship*
- *Career*

Flow

- *Essentials*
- *Non-Essentials*
- *Value-based spending*

50/20/30 (Budgeting Style)

- *50 Needs (Things you need to survive)*
- *30%: Wants (Things you want to buy)*
- *20%: Savings (Investing in yourself)*

OUR MONEY STORIES | 153

OUR MONEY STORIES | 153

Step 3: Put bills and statements in files.

Print out your bills. I know that this may seem crazy, but you have to print out your invoices. At least at first. For all my tech people that refuse to get a file cabinet, print out your bills annually, having at least one printed paycheck stub and statements so that you can go back.

*Note if you are a freelancer, entrepreneur, or work for the gig economy (Lyfte, Task Rabbit).

You would have to be more diligent with printing out your payments in the first three years. I did every job under the sun, especially when I first decided to get into financial planning. I once worked for a CEO named Shalimar Thomas, who was working on revitalizing a neighbor while I was in graduate school. What I noticed was that Shalimar printed out every invoice and paystubs. I was so against doing this, but then I saw how grounded she was in her organization, so I started mimicking her. When you track, you know.

Step 4: Monitor Bank/Credit Card Activity

Print out your bank and credit card statement. Tracking is key to monitoring. While some people only use cash, we live in a tech society; most people use credit cards and bank cards to purchase things. It means looking at your bank check monthly activity and seeing where your money goes. Depending on where you are with your mental health, it can be a challenge, and there will be times where you'll forget, but you know what will remind you? Your file cabinet that's collecting dust.

When you are looking at your bank activity, start looking for three things:

1. Essential Items- Needs.

2. Non-essential Items-Wants.

3. Investing.

1) Essential Items

Maslow's Hierarchy of Needs is so crucial to your life. If your basic needs aren't met, you can be pretending to live your best life, but crying behind closed doors. Do you have rent, phone, and mental health bills? All of your needs are in this budget. If you have children, you include them in the needs pile.

- Groceries

- Housing

- Utilities

- Health insurance

- Car payment

- Student Loans Wants

2) Non-Essential Items

Do you want to take a trip to Thailand? Or get a stitch fix subscription? You can have some fun with your funds. You can spend money on whatever you want. The problem with a lot of budgets is we forget actually to add fun to it.

- Shopping

- Dining Out

- Hobbies
- Subscriptions
- Holidays

3) Investing

Where you invest in your future self. You take your amount and invest in your future. It's essential to have this portion in your life because you are telling your future self that you believe in them. You track your:

- Roth IRA
- 403b
- 401k
- Resume building to get a new job

Step 4: For all your money activity, do the following for each purchase.

1. Circle all the essential Items (bills, rent)
2. Underline all of the non-essential items (Shopping, Dining Out, etc)
3. Place a checkmark by your investments

Step 5:

Add up all your spending (Use a Calculator) and ask the question:

How much every month am I spending on my essential items?

How much every month am I spending on my non-essential items?

Add up all your Investing (Use a Calculator) basic needs and ask the question:

How much every month am I spending on my investments?

Step 6: Write Out Money Narrative

Your money story is about tracking the habit of you. Answer the following questions:

How do I feel after following my money?

What is one thing that I'm proud of when tracking my money?

What is one area where I wish to improve?

Chapter 30
Week 5: Your Net Worth

Alright, we're on to week five! What a journey it has been. I'm so proud of you for making a change. In week five, we are going to look at your net-worth! For some folks, net worth can feel overwhelming. This makes sense because the only net worth that we mostly hear about are those of wealthy people. It's essential to look at the numbers because we have to be our advocates.

In this portion of the book, we look at:

1. What is Net Worth?

2. My Net Worth (The time I've written this book)

3. Breaking Down Your Net Worth

4. Your Credit Score

Before we get started, I must state these relevant statements

Your Net Worth is Not Your Self Worth

Your Net worth is not Your Network.

I have to say this because this week can try to test you and make you feel less than. It can also make you rethink friendships and relationships. As mentioned in the entire book, this is a journey.

What is Net worth?

Net worth is a number that determines where you stand with your money. According to Bankrate, the Net worth is the value of all assets, minus the total of all liabilities. Net worth is a part of the financial wellness process because it says what you would have leftover if all your assets could pay all of your debts this minute.

Here are examples of Assets are something you own:

- Home
- Cars (no car note)
- Collectables
- Household items (furniture, electronics, etc.)
- Retirement (401k, 403b, Roth IRA, IRA)
- Investments (stocks, bonds, mutual funds)
- Jewelry
- Cash- Checking and Savings

Liabilities are the things that you owe. That may be in the form of:

- Auto loans
- Student loans
- Credit Card Debt

- Other loans

- House mortgage

Assets- Liabilities= Net worth

What's the difference between income and net worth?

Profit is how much you make every month to pay your bills and invest. Net worth is where you stand with paying off debts right now.

Why is knowing Your Net worth important?

Your net worth is essential because you can see where you stand with your money. It's also necessary to know what you own. Lastly, if you are purchasing a home, putting away for retirement, or just saving for a rainy day, it's a constant reminder that YOU KNOW where you stand with your money.

My Net Worth Story

There's nothing like music to your ears when you open up your email, and there's a friendly reminder from Mohela that your student loan payment is due SOON. When I say music, I mean horror music. I knew that it was time for me to be transparent with my numbers, and I also was at the beginning of writing this book that I wanted to be as truthful as possible.

DEBT. Let's talk about it. I owe people money. I want to celebrate some wins before I show you my new debts. Now, to my net worth. During the time of this first release of Our Money Stories. My net worth is -$75,625 (2019). It is a number that I cried about some time with my financial planner Kristy Runzer, but as she continually reminds me, most people have a negative net worth at all times. I'm becoming a Financial Planner, and I am building social capital by building a business and learning about finances.

I wanted to let you know that it's okay if you're in the negative. Now, what makes my money story different and yours too is that we know our numbers. From this plan, we are taking active steps to change our narrative. So, when I look at my student loans, I don't call it debt anymore, I call it a personal growth fund. I know that the loans I took out for graduate school have helped me write this book, and live. I knew that getting an MBA would help me with my future self. I knew that taking a year off of the real world to figure out how to build wealth and understand my mental health was crucial to my narrative, although it was painful at times.

Calculating Your Net Worth

Step 1: Gather data

I want you to find and make two piles

Pile One: Everything that you owe (liability)

Pile Two: Everything that you own (asset)

Here's a quick review of the assets and liabilities

Assets are something you own	Liabilities are the cost that you owe.
• Home • cars • Collectables • Household items (furniture, electronics, etc.) • Retirement (401k, 403b, Roth IRA, IRA) • Investments (stocks, bonds, mutual funds) • Jewelry • Cash- Checking's and Savings	• Auto loans • Student loans • Credit Card Debt • Auto Loans • House mortgage • Personal Loans

Step 2: Calculate Your Net-worth

Here's an example:

This is Julissa. She's got a great career in tech. She was the first to attend college in her family and is an activist. Let's calculate her net-worth

Assets are something you own	Liabilities are the cost that you owe. That may be in form of
• Home	
• Cars (4,000)	• Auto loans $
• Household items: Her Apartment is 1,000	• Student loans 12,000
• Retirement (401k, 403b, Roth IRA, IRA) 4,000	• Credit Card Debt $1,000
	• Other loans
• Jewelry	• House mortgage
• Cash- Checking and Savings	**12,000+1,000= 13,000**
Total Assets 4,000 + 1,000+ 4,000 = 9,000	**Total Liabilities= -13,000**
Total Assets= 9,000	

Assets- Liabilities= Net worth

9,000 -13,000= - 4,000

Now, it's your turn:

Step 3: Calculate Your Net Worth

Step 4: Write out Your Net Worth

My net-worth is?

How do I feel after calculating my net worth?

What is one thing that I'm proud of when tracking my money?

Step 5: Find Your Credit Score

What do Emma Stone and Credit Score have in common?

They were both introduced into the world in 1989. That's right. Credit Scores are Millennials. So, before we dive into credit scores. I just want y'all to know that credit is a baby and it is always a work in progress. That being said, let's dive into it.

We live in a society where a FICO score can affect your everyday life. From purchasing a car to taking out student loans. Credit is defined as the ability to purchase products ahead of time and ensure the lender that you will pay them back what you owe. A Lannister always pays their debts, but what happens when a Lannister has a credit card? Or student loans?

What is a Credit Score?

Credit scores are a mathematical formula that shoots out a number from all the data collected onto your credit report. This score determines an important factor. According to the *Consumer Financial Protection Bureau*, the elements that make up a typical credit score include:

- Your bill-paying history

- Your current unpaid debt

- The number and type of loan accounts you have

- How long you have had your loan accounts open

- How much of your available credit you are currently using

- New applications for credit

- Whether you have had a debt sent to collection, a foreclosure, or a bankruptcy, and how long ago.[cxxxi]

It's important to note that credit scores aren't just one score. Multiple companies have scoring systems, but the most trusted ones are Equifax, Experian, and TransUnion. Your credit scores show your history, and people can make life-long decisions to your social and economic opportunities. For most of us, we established a credit history using our student loans. You can use rent, credit cards, student, and home loans to utilize your credit score.

Discrimination

The score itself is not a problem; it was still an issue of class and wealth. Your credit history can decide if you get a job, house, insurance, and loans. Credit reports don't factor how discrimination works. There were already inequalities within our system to begin with; then, your credit score can serve as a proxy. If your parents chose to help you, you had fewer problems with understanding how and why credit is necessary.

For some of us, we received credit scores through credit cards when we started college or turned 18 years old because, until 2009, it was the wild wild west of credit cards. It was like Oprah's Favorite Things. You get a credit card! I remember having a credit card, spending it on pointless things, and having a 1,000 bill in the mail, and I was unable to pay for it. I would go to my family, and they were unable to pay it either. It was because, before the CARD Act of 2009, 18-year-olds could get as many credit cards as they wanted, without the education of credit scoring. The law requires that, unless the applicant has a substantial income, adults under 21 must have a cosigner to get a credit card.[cxxxii] I don't want to get into all the discrimination that has occurred because this is our get it done part of the book.

Grab your Free Credit Report.

By law, we are allowed to have three free detailed credit reports. If you pay, they are asking you to pay for an annual subscription. The way that Credit Scores play into your money story is that it is an investment in your future. Your money and your future are essential, and sure you might have made mistakes in the past, but your credit score is a number. Don't get overwhelmed with the score. Include your score in your budgeting plan because it can help you determine where you want to spot ways to save- for free and build for the future.

Step 4: Place in Your Folder Your Net-worth and Credit Report

Step 5: Look at the schedule and see if your Money Date works

Step 6: Treat yo Self

Chapter 31

Week 6: Money Brain Dumps and Money Goals

We made it to the last week of your financial wellness plan. In this plan, we'll look at

1. Money Brain Dumps

2. Asking the Question: What does it look to be financially well?

3. Setting financial goals

Money Brain Dump 101

A Money Brain Dump is transferring a large quantity of information from your brain to paper. In school, it was called Brainstorming. A Brain Dump is useful for all those nagging thoughts you might have. I recommend doing a Money Brain Dump every month. This way, you have a running list of all the things you need. Let's dig into it!

Step 1: Take a piece of paper out and set a 5-10 timer

Make a list of all the ideas that are running through your mind about money. Just get the ideas flowing. If you need a cup of coffee or good music, do that. Make an on-going list.

Step 2: Ask the question: What does it mean to be financially well to me?

Here we're going to take a deep dive into our financial wellness pillars. They were mentioned before in Chapter 30. As you look at the posts, what is the number one pillar that you would like to focus on for the next 90 days?

Step 3: Answer this question

If I could focus on one pillar this month, what would it be?

How would it help your Money brain dump and your spending?

Step 4: Congratulate Yourself

Step 5: Schedule those Money Dates for the next week

Part Four

FINANCIAL
BFF 101

CHAPTER 32
FINANCIAL BFF 101 + NOW WHAT

We just moved from not knowing how our ancestors can affect our money story to having an action plan to tackle these money questions. The 6-week action plan can be a lot. We went from looking at big picture ideas to detailing our thoughts.

At the end of this book, I want to equip you with the necessary tools you need to fully understand your money story. I want you to be able to take these money ideas, keep them in your money toolbox, and be able to refer to them when you need them, and with confidence.

Why do we need Financial BFFs?

Financial BFFs are our community, support, and mentors to help us with our money stories. We all need money support groups because we don't know what we don't know. Plus, we gain more confidence in all aspects of our lives when we know where and how our money is coming in.

During my money story journey, I didn't realize how many people were helping me along the way. When I met up with Sonia Lewis, the Student Loan Doctor, and we looked at my student loans, and it turned out wasn't worth the stress because I had consistently paid off my student loans.

Then I spoke to Joe Holberg of Holberg Financial, and he told me not to sweat and focus on the positives. When I drew out my financial plan with my partner, Kristy Runzer On Route Financial, she helped me keep my cool with my man. When I got a branding consultant, Antoinette Minor of TYP Social, she taught me how to save money on my business with social media. I interacted with my accountant for life Erica Booth Accounting. She made me feel okay about where I was with, both personally and professionally. Lastly, whenever I need a dose of having a seat at the table, I get my daily dose of Minda Hart, from The Memo. The ability to look at the big picture with an accountability partner is essential.

How does this help you with your action plan?

When you are in the process of getting your financial life together, you will have questions and goals that you want to accomplish—this clear guide of who can help you and some valuable resources along the way.

CHAPTER 33
BEHAVIORAL AND HABIT
CHANGING BFFS

According to science, the amount of time it takes to change a habit is 66 days, which is around ten weeks. Almost an entire season. Which is why it's crazy that this "get rich" scheme allows people to change their habits in a month. Heck, even my six weeks is always teasing the problem. It's because when things are hard, our brain tells us we all look for quick- options to release the pain in our minds.

We all need to identify our habits with someone who we don't have a close relationship with. Having someone with a non-bias view does not help identify buried patterns through our money story, but they help us find our money strengths. In this book, there are six different types of people that help you with just changing the behavior of your money thoughts.

1. Debtors Anonymous

2. Credit Repair Coaches

3. Financial Coach

4. Financial Therapist/ Counselor

5. Money Coach

6. Financial Educators

Debtor's/ Underearners Anonymous

What happens when you can't stop spending, and your life is all over the place? You've gone to family and friends, and they can't help you out anymore. Many of us have experienced it, but each is unique. Debtor/ Underearners Anonymous is a non-judgmental environment where you can have group therapy through a 12- step program. The basic idea of a 12-step program is if you are struggling with an addiction (working, alcohol, etc.), you can follow a process to help you manage your problems.

The ultimate goals for these programs are to help you admit that you are powerless with your spending, analyze yourself and behaviors, and find your higher purpose. The end goal is to stop incurring debt. This group approach is very successful with women. According to a study from the Journal of Substance Abuse Treatment, going to the 12-step programs involves "cognitive restructuring – or the ability to change thought patterns in ways that also change behavior." – It is an essential element of substance abuse treatment.[cxxxiii]

Now, we don't know the scientific benefits of attending a money treatment, but what we do know is that all money group coaching programs are the direct spawn of Debtors Anonymous. Heck, even Jenny Craig, is based on a group support business model. Working in groups can dramatically help your process.

The D.A. and U.A. are helping you play the long game...

A very successful friend of mine told me about it. I was in complete shock. How could my 6-figure, married to a beautiful man attend a 12-group program? She told me that the group helps her become okay with her debt. She said D.A. helped her stop underselling herself when it comes to her business. Plus, the group aspects brought her to more business owners, and that helped her increase her profits, to recognize her behaviors, but this took a lot of work and years, but the program is Free99.

Requirements and Training: The group meetings are free, and anyone can host a call. To help people with their debt one-on-one basis has completed the 12-step program or has not accrued additional debt.

Glows: It's a free in-person, phone, or virtual experience. You have the flexibility to come and go in the program.

Things to be aware of: It takes time to get over your money trauma. Sometimes, you might find it hard to discover a community that sticks. BEWARE of energy vampires. Some people use these platforms to prey on people.

Credit Repair

Credit Repair coaches and companies work on eliminating negative credit information. They look for errors and help you build your credit. Many times, people come to credit coaches when they are ready to purchase a home, apply for an apartment, or make a life-changing push for their money story. These credit repairs come in all shapes and sizes.

Glows: They help you with one task. Credit Repair companies are also helpful as a habit changer and have great people that only focus on this task.

Areas of Growth: You have to be careful because some credit repair folks can rip you out of your money. Knowing their money story might be beneficial.

Financial Coaching

Financial coaching is an appropriate step to take to uncover your behavior habits. The majority of people find financial coaches when they read personal finance columns or through a connection. Financial literacy is on the rise, and most financial coaches have overarching themes to help people which include:

- Build self- Awareness of money story

- Look at your spending habits

- Create confidence around budgeting

- Help you dream a different lifestyle

- Look at behaviors

- Help you build savings plans (CFPB)

Requirements and Training: It's important to note that financial coaching isn't regulated. It's essential to ask specific questions. There is one nationally recognized leader in financial coaching, which is the Association for Financial Counseling & Planning Education® (AFCPE®).

Glows: There are a variety of options depending on the business model or coach. The coaching styles vary.

Financial coaching provides one on one interaction. Some people charge up to 2,000, and some people cost around 97 dollars.

Things to be aware of: If a Financial Coach is telling you to purchase money in stocks or spending money in a particular place, you have to check this advice and see if it's sound.

Financial Counselor

Similar to Financial coaching, Financial counselors help people understand the basics of money. Financial Counselors, listen and focus on the client and guide them to understand the big picture of their debt. They also help you create a realistic savings plan. They provide you with tools if a bill is unpaid.

Financial counselors tend to have extensive in-depth knowledge of the financial difficulties of folks that are middle to low-income households. You may find financial counselors on college campuses, as well as working at non-profit organizations. Some counselors are in the form of student loan companies. The goals for financial counselors help people get out of debt, build up an emergency fund, and catch up on bills that have gone unpaid.[cxxxiv]

Requirements and Training:

There isn't a requirement to become a financial counsellor. If a counselor wanted to deepen their practice, they could get an Association for Financial Counseling & Planning Education® (AFCPE®). AFC® certification is the standard — training professionals to guide clients through life-cycle financial education to help them realize their goals and achieve lasting economic well-being.

Glows: If they are (AFCPE®) or AFC® certified, their certification is recognized by all governmental organizations as sound practices.

Things to be aware of: Nada

Money Coach

If you need to think big like Oprah, then a Money Coach is likely to be right up to your alley. Most money coaches help you focus on making more money. The money coaching community is very convoluted. Some folks help with saving and paying down debt, and others are former business coaches who have changed their name. There is a time and a place for money coaches. Educators need a relentless push to manifest money.

Requirements and Training: There are not any requirements but look at the money coaches' credentials. Do they have a successful money blog? Do they have a successful business practice? Find out. Prices vary.

Glows: Most of the money coaches are direct with their results.

Items to be mindful of: Their methods may not work for you.

Financial Educators

Most personal finance gurus operate as Financial educators. Any YouTube influencers or personal finance bloggers fall into this category. They are not allowed to provide you with advice; they are providing you with their own opinion. Financial educators are Dave

Ramsey's, David Bachs, and Suze Orman's. Financial educators have the goal to help you get out of debt, think about retirement, and help you think about your savings. Financial educators provide step-by-step instructions, or they tell you how to use their techniques to help you achieve the same success as they have.

Requirement and Training:

Not required to have training. It can be anyone because they are educating people about money not managing people's money.

Glows: Let's be real, without Financial Educators; regular folks wouldn't get any money information. It's because the financial industry caters to high-net-worth.

Things to be aware of: The dilemma with educators isn't that they are doing something wrong, it's that most folks follow their ideas as if it is the holy grail of finance, and that is not the case. Without financial educators, most people wouldn't have access to financial advice.

Requirements and Training: No training is required. There are certified financial educator certifications.

Chapter 34
The Licensed BFFs

For some Financial BFFs, a season isn't enough; some require a lifelong process. These are what I call the licensed ones. In this book, there are six different types of people that help you with just changing the behavior of your money thoughts.

1. Financial Therapist

2. Financial Adviser/ Advisor

3. Certified Financial Planners CFP

4. CFA-Chartered Financial Analyst

5. Accountant and Certified Public Accountant

Financial Therapist

Financial therapy is used to uncover all your money habits whilst in a safe environment. Emerging out of traditional therapy and better ways to help financial planners understand the real truth behind their client's spending habits. The co-founder of the Association of Financial Therapists, Kristy Archuleta, explains that F.T., an individual, brain-based, looks at how to deal with social systems and how people interact with social networks.[cxxxv] It's different from other plans because there is no one size fits all model. They also recognize that to provide advice, giving people a list is not an excellent way to improve financial behaviors.

Requirements and Training: It depends; most people are either trained therapists that specialize in financial therapy or financial planners that want to help understand their client's money identity. The center of Financial Therapy is emerging, and they offer The Certified Financial Therapist-I™ (CFT-I™) designation will be a professional certification for both financial and mental health professionals conferred by the Financial Therapy Association.

Glow: All and all, people are required to have hundreds of hours of therapy practice. You can also use your therapist to talk about money habits.

Things do be aware of: Financial therapy is new, and not every therapist will have the cultural competence to understand your money story.

Financial Adviser/ Advisor[cxxxvi][cxxxvii]

If you are thinking about building wealth, you will hear the word adviser or advisor thrown around a lot. Both are different. When we look at the big picture of a Financial Adviser or Advisor, they both want to help you build wealth and think about retirement. Both professionals suggest or advise financial services based on the client's money situation. The difference is the methodology and laws behind each of their actions.

An adviser is someone who is registered under the SEC as a Registered Investment Adviser. F.A. is not holding up the fiduciary code, then the adviser will be put on blast, and they pay attention to if you are defrauding the clients.

Requirements and Training: It depends on the advice. They all require licensing and training. With few exceptions, broker-dealers must register with the Securities and Exchange Commission (SEC) and be members of FINRA. Still, they can register with the SEC or state depending on the situation.

Glows: Advisers or Advisors are a person or company that is in the business of buying and selling securities— stocks, bonds, mutual funds, and certain other investment products—on behalf of its customers (as a broker) for its account (as a dealer) or both.[cxxxviii]

Things to be aware of: Uh, not all financial advisors are created equal. For years they sold the wrong stocks, which is why we had the Recession and Depression. They can also be in a bubble to get a commission from their sales.

CFA-Chartered Financial Analyst

A CFA is an investor that looks at ethical standards when it comes to trading stocks, creating investment analysis, and portfolios. They focus on the future of markets as well as government regulation—the ability to report on financial operation systems debt and global operations.

Training and Requirements: There are three exams that they must pass. Each level up from the previous one. You must have four years of real-life work experience within the industry to take the exam.

Glows: If you talk to a CFA, they are unicorns in the game

Things to be aware of: There are not many CFA's that specialize in regular folks, which means most high net worth.

Accountant[cxxxix]

The art of accounting is the ability to report business and financial transactions. Think of your student body treasurer in high school; what did they even do?

They paid attention to where the money for homecoming went, and it was real money. The accountant pays attention to financial transactions.

- Examines statements to ensure accuracy

- Ensures that reports and records comply with laws and regulations

- Computes taxes owed, prepare tax returns, ensure prompt payment

- Inspects account books and accounting systems to keep up to date

- Organizes and maintain financial records

- Improves businesses efficiency where the money is concerned

- Makes best-practices recommendations to management

- Suggests ways to reduce costs, enhance revenues and improve profits

- Provides auditing services for businesses and individuals

Certified Public Accountant[cxl]

There is a difference between a CPA and Accountant, and it all boils down to experience and training. CPA looks at audited, reviewed, and compiled financial statements, typically they work for corporations. Accountants work with individuals and small businesses.

Glows: They can both be with you in all aspects of your life.

Things to be aware of: Read the descriptions before you schedule an appointment

CFP- Certified Financial Planner[cxli]

A Certified Financial Planner is a person that helps a client to address their full financial landscape. It's the gold standard of financial planning. They help you with insurance, investments, estate, retirement, and much more. The difference between an advisor or a Financial Coach is that by law, the CFP must help based on the client's interests and not on their own. For example, if the client didn't want life insurance, you don't push them to get it.

Training and requirements: Like the CFA and CPA, you must take additional classes and courses. You must be eligible to receive the test with either taking the CFP exam, and you must have work experience in finance. You have to take a two-day exam and pass like the law bar for money.

Glows: they can see the financial life cycle—so many different niche planners. The cost varies. A couple of organizations have a list that serves to find financial planners that are right for you.

Things to be aware of: Some are Fee-only. Meaning, they will charge you a flat fee for advice.

Some are commission-based.

Last Words 2020
(Before COVID-19)

I hope you enjoyed the book. Writing this book was a great experience. As I was in the process of editing this book, Coronavirus hit the globe. There is a global shift towards creating a more inclusive environment, but as the world is changing, note that your old patterns are still lingering. It's time to shed some of the past to create a better future.

Bonus

Would you like a printed out copy of your Six Week Financial Wellness Plan? Grab Your Free 35-page worksheet

Included is all 6 Week Exercises

Log on to
https://eugeniegeorge.com/financialwellnessplan

Passcode: Ancestral

WORK CITED

[i] Barr, S. (2016, December 21). What's Your Money Story? Retrieved May 31, 2020, from http://sheroldbarr.com/whats-your-money-story/

[ii] Hayden, B. (2014, March 20). I Had Been Fired and Evicted, and Still Retired at 27. Retrieved May 31, 2020, from https://www.entrepreneur.com/article/232341

[iii] Desmond, M. (2014, March). *Poor Black Women Are Evicted at Alarming Rates, Setting Off a Chain of Hardship* [Scholarly project]. In *How Housing Matters*. Retrieved from https://www.macfound.org/media/files/HHM_Research _Brief_- _Poor_Black_Women_Are_Evicted_at_Alarming_Rate s.pdf

[iv] Jones, A. (2017, June 20). Entrepreneur strives to empower Philly students with financial education. Retrieved May 31, 2020, from https://www.phillytrib.com/news/entrepreneur-strives- to-empower-philly-students-with-financial- education/article_85a42e90-e258-5a14-9636- 5e6ee6a33237.html

[v] James, J. W., & Cherry, F. (1989). *The grief recovery handbook: A step-by-step program for moving beyond loss*. New York: Harper & Row.

[vi] Holden, K. B., Bradford, L. D., Hall, S. P., & Belton, A. S. (2014). Prevalence and Correlates of Depressive Symptoms and Resiliency among African American Women in a Community-Based Primary Health Care Center. *Journal of Health Care for the Poor and Underserved*, *24*(4A), 79-93. doi:10.1353/hpu.2014.0012

[vii] Dweck, C. S. (2007). *Is Math a Gift? Beliefs That Put Females at Risk.* In S. J. Ceci & W. M. Williams (Eds.), *Why aren't more women in science?: Top researchers debate the evidence* (p. 47–55). American Psychological Association. https://doi.org/10.1037/11546-004

[viii] Barseghian, T. (2012, January 10). Girls and Math: Busting the Stereotype. Retrieved May 31, 2020, from https://www.kqed.org/mindshift/18057/girls-and-math-busting-the-stereotype

[ix] Tripett, K. (2017, November 09). Rachel Yehuda - How Trauma and Resilience Cross Generations. Retrieved May 31, 2020, from https://onbeing.org/programs/rachel-yehuda-how-trauma-and-resilience-cross-generations-nov2017/

[x]Rodriguez, T. (2015, March 01). Descendants of Holocaust Survivors Have Altered Stress Hormones.

Retrieved May 31, 2020, from
https://www.scientificamerican.com/article/descendants
-of-holocaust-survivors-have-altered-stress-hormones/

[xi] Rodriguez, T. (2015, March 01). Descendants of
Holocaust Survivors Have Altered Stress Hormones.
Retrieved May 31, 2020, from
https://www.scientificamerican.com/article/descendants
-of-holocaust-survivors-have-altered-stress-hormones/

[xii] Yasmin, S. (2019, August 25). No, trauma is not
inherited. Retrieved May 31, 2020, from
https://www.dallasnews.com/news/2017/05/30/no-
trauma-is-not-inherited/

[xiii] Duhigg, C. (2012). The **Power of Habit**: Why we do
what we do in life and business. New York: Random
House.

[xiv] Patton, S. (2017). *In Spare the Kids: Why Whupping
Children Won't Save Black America,*.

[xv] *Racial Disproportionality and Disparity in Child
Welfare* [Pamphlet]. (2015). Washington, DC: Children's
Bureau.

[xvi] Patton, PHd, S. (2017). Corporal punishment in black
communities: Not an intrinsic cultural tradition but racial

trauma. Retrieved May 31, 2020, from https://www.apa.org/pi/families/resources/newsletter/20 17/04/racial-trauma

[xvii] Nudd, T. (2009, November 06). Rihanna gives painful details of Chris Brown assault. Retrieved May 31, 2020, from https://www.cnn.com/2009/SHOWBIZ/Music/11/06/riha nna.chris.brown/index.html

[xviii] Evans, K. (2017, April 11). How about sparing the kid and not using the rod? Retrieved May 31, 2020, from https://theundefeated.com/features/how-about-sparing-the-kid-and-not-using-the-rod/

[xix] Center for Disease Control. (2020, April 03). Adverse Childhood Experiences (ACEs). Retrieved May 31, 2020, from https://www.cdc.gov/violenceprevention/childabuseand neglect/acestudy/index.html

[xx] Stevens, J. (2018, November 02). To prevent childhood trauma, pediatricians screen children and their parents...and sometimes, just parents...for childhood trauma. Retrieved May 31, 2020, from https://acestoohigh.com/2014/07/29/to-prevent-childhood-trauma-pediatricians-screen-children-and-their-parentsand-sometimes-just-parents/

[xxi] Stevens, J. (2015, June 03). The Adverse Childhood Experiences Study - the largest, most important public health study you never heard of - began in an obesity clinic. Retrieved May 31, 2020, from https://acestoohigh.com/2012/10/03/the-adverse-childhood-experiences-study-the-largest-most-important-public-health-study-you-never-heard-of-began-in-an-obesity-clinic/

[xxii] Stevens, J. (2015, June 03). The Adverse Childhood Experiences Study - the largest, most important public health study you never heard of - began in an obesity clinic. Retrieved May 31, 2020, from https://acestoohigh.com/2012/10/03/the-adverse-childhood-experiences-study-the-largest-most-important-public-health-study-you-never-heard-of-began-in-an-obesity-clinic/

[xxiii] Stevens, J. (2015, June 03). The Adverse Childhood Experiences Study - the largest, most important public health study you never heard of - began in an obesity clinic. Retrieved May 31, 2020, from https://acestoohigh.com/2012/10/03/the-adverse-childhood-experiences-study-the-largest-most-important-public-health-study-you-never-heard-of-began-in-an-obesity-clinic/

[xxiv] Harris, N. (n.d.). How childhood trauma affects health across a lifetime. Retrieved May 31, 2020, from

https://www.ted.com/talks/nadine_burke_harris_how_
childhood_trauma_affects_health_across_a_lifetime

[xxv] Home: Money and Mental Health Policy Institute - a
charity founded by Martin Lewis. (2020, May 18).
Retrieved May 31, 2020, from
https://www.moneyandmentalhealth.org/

[xxvi] Elizabeth's Consumer Financial Protection Bureau is
Standing Up For American Consumers and Holding Wall
Street Accountable. (2019, August 19). Retrieved May 31,
2020, from https://facts.elizabethwarren.com/cfpb/

[xxvii] Killman, C. (2019, July 07). Day 1: Breaking the cycle.
Retrieved May 31, 2020, from
https://www.tulsaworld.com/day-breaking-the-
cycle/article_e34e5228-ff35-5a98-b342-
937c7e06d373.html

[xxviii] Killman, C. (2019, July 07). Day 1: Breaking the
cycle. Retrieved May 31, 2020, from
https://www.tulsaworld.com/day-breaking-the-
cycle/article_e34e5228-ff35-5a98-b342-
937c7e06d373.html

[xxix] Killman, C. (2019, July 07). Day 1: Breaking the cycle.
Retrieved May 31, 2020, from
https://www.tulsaworld.com/day-breaking-the-

cycle/article_e34e5228-ff35-5a98-b342-
937c7e06d373.html

[xxx] Killman, C. (2019, July 07). Day 1: Breaking the cycle.
Retrieved May 31, 2020, from
https://www.tulsaworld.com/day-breaking-the-
cycle/article_e34e5228-ff35-5a98-b342-
937c7e06d373.html

[xxxi] Japanese Immigration. (2018, September 12).
Retrieved May 31, 2020, from
https://americanhistory.si.edu/righting-wrong-japanese-
americans-and-world-war-ii/japanese-immigration

[xxxii][xxxii] Nott, J. C., Gliddon, G. R., Morton, S. G., Agassiz,
L., Usher, W., & Patterson, H. S. (1854). *Types of
mankind: Or Ethnological researches, based upon the
ancient monuments, paintings, sculptures, and crania of
races, and upon their natural, geographical, philological,
and biblical history: Illustrated by selections from the
inedited papers of Samuel George Morton, and by
additional contributions from L. Agassiz, W. Usher, and
H.S. Patterson*. Philadelphia: Lippincott, Grambo &.

[xxxiii] Chinese Exclusion Act. (n.d.). Retrieved May 31,
2020, from
http://encyclopedia.densho.org/Chinese_Exclusion_Act
/

[xxxiv] History.com Staff. (2018, August 24). Chinese Exclusion Act. Retrieved May 31, 2020, from https://www.history.com/topics/immigration/chinese-exclusion-act-1882

[xxxv] National Archives. (1989). Home. Retrieved May 31, 2020, from https://www.ourdocuments.gov/doc.php?flash=false

[xxxvi] Bonilla-Silva, E. (2014). *Racism without racists: color-blind racism and the persistence of racial inequality in America.* Fourth edition. Lanham: Rowman & Littlefield Publishers, Inc.

[xxxvii] History.com Editors. (2009, October 29). Japanese Internment Camps. Retrieved May 31, 2020, from https://www.history.com/topics/world-war-ii/japanese-american-relocation

[xxxviii] Weller, C., & Thompson, J. (n.d.). Wealth Inequality Among Asian Americans Greater Than Among Whites. Retrieved May 31, 2020, from https://www.americanprogress.org/issues/race/reports/2016/12/20/295359/wealth-inequality-among-asian-americans-greater-than-among-whites/

[xxxix][xxxix][xxxix] Weller, C. (2018, September 18). Despite Successful Minority Stereotype, Asian-Americans Face Worse Retirement Crisis Than Whites. Retrieved May

31, 2020, from
https://www.forbes.com/sites/christianweller/2018/09/18
/retirement-crisis-worse-for-asian-americans-than-
whites/

[xl] Budiman, A. (2020, May 07). Asian Americans are the
fastest-growing racial or ethnic group in the U.S.
electorate. Retrieved May 31, 2020, from
https://www.pewresearch.org/fact-
tank/2020/05/07/asian-americans-are-the-fastest-
growing-racial-or-ethnic-group-in-the-u-s-electorate/

[xli] Lim, B. (2015). The Effects of Seeing Asian-Americans
as a 'Model Minority'. Retrieved May 31, 2020, from
https://www.nytimes.com/roomfordebate/2015/10/16/the
-effects-of-seeing-asian-americans-as-a-model-
minority/model-minority-seems-like-a-compliment-
but-it-does-great-harm

[xlii] Chen, S. (2018, May 10). Racial Wealth Snapshot:
Asian Americans. Retrieved May 31, 2020, from
https://prosperitynow.org/blog/racial-wealth-snapshot-
asian-americans

[xliii] Chen, S. (2018, May 10). Racial Wealth Snapshot:
Asian Americans. Retrieved May 31, 2020, from
https://prosperitynow.org/blog/racial-wealth-snapshot-
asian-americans

[xliv] Equal Pay Day. (2019). Equal Pay Today! Retrieved May 31, 2020, from http://www.equalpaytoday.org/

[xlv] SOONLING BLACKBURN, S. (2019). What Is the Model Minority Myth? Retrieved May 31, 2020, from https://www.tolerance.org/magazine/what-is-the-model-minority-myth

[xlvi][xlvi] Nishi, MA, K. (2019). Mental Health Among Asian-Americans. Retrieved May 31, 2020, from https://www.apa.org/pi/oema/resources/ethnicity-health/asian-american/article-mental-health

[xlvii] Lee, S., Edelman, M., Rogers, B., Morial, M., Ueberroth, P., Tutu, D., & NIchols, R. (2019). Freedman's Bank. Retrieved May 31, 2020, from http://freedmansbank.org/

[xlviii] The Freedman's Savings and Trust Company and African American Genealogical Research. (2017). Retrieved May 31, 2020, from https://www.archives.gov/publications/prologue/1997/summer/freedmans-savings-and-trust.html

[xlix][xlix] The Freedman's Savings and Trust Company and African American Genealogical Research. (2017). Retrieved May 31, 2020, from https://www.archives.gov/publications/prologue/1997/summer/freedmans-savings-and-trust.html

[l] The Freedman's Savings and Trust Company and African American Genealogical Research. (2017). Retrieved May 31, 2020, from https://www.archives.gov/publications/prologue/1997/summer/freedmans-savings-and-trust.html

[li][li] The Freedman's Bank: A Story of Faith, Family and Finance. (2017). Retrieved May 31, 2020, from https://www.clevelandfed.org/en/learningcenter/exhibits/freedmans-bank.aspx

[lii] The Freedman's Bank: A Story of Faith, Family and Finance. (2017). Retrieved May 31, 2020, from https://www.clevelandfed.org/en/learningcenter/exhibits/freedmans-bank.aspx

[liii][liii] Lee, S., Edelman, M., Rogers, B., Morial, M., Ueberroth, P., Tutu, D., & NIchols, R. (2017). Freedman's Bank. Retrieved May 31, 2020, from http://freedmansbank.org/

[liv] Peck, G. (2013). The Smithsonian Castle and The Seneca Quarry (Landmarks ... Retrieved May 31, 2020, from https://www.amazon.com/Smithsonian-Castle-Seneca-Quarry-Landmarks/dp/1609499298

[lv][lv] Lee, S., Edelman, M., Rogers, B., Morial, M., Ueberroth, P., Tutu, D., & NIchols, R. (2017). Freedman's

Bank. Retrieved May 31, 2020, from
http://freedmansbank.org/

[lvi] Nunn, S. (2017, August 06). Black-Owned Banks Hit
Their Peak a Century Ago. Retrieved May 31, 2020, from
https://www.wsj.com/articles/black-owned-banks-hit-
their-peak-a-century-ago-1502020802

[lvii] Clark, A. (2019, September 04). Tulsa's 'Black Wall
Street' Flourished as a Self-Contained Hub in Early
1900s. Retrieved May 31, 2020, from
https://www.history.com/news/black-wall-street-tulsa-
race-massacre

[lviii] The History of Black Wall Street: America's Largest
Black Owned Bank. (2017, February 27). Retrieved May
31, 2020, from https://www.oneunited.com/the-history-
of-black-wall-street/

[lix] The History of Black Wall Street: America's Largest
Black Owned Bank. (2017, February 27). Retrieved May
31, 2020, from https://www.oneunited.com/the-history-
of-black-wall-street/

[lx] History.com Editors. (2018, March 08). Tulsa Race
Massacre. Retrieved May 31, 2020, from
https://www.history.com/topics/roaring-twenties/tulsa-
race-massacre

[lxi] History.com Editors. (2018, March 08). Tulsa Race Massacre. Retrieved May 31, 2020, from https://www.history.com/topics/roaring-twenties/tulsa-race-massacre

[lxii] History.com Editors. (2018, March 08). Tulsa Race Massacre. Retrieved May 31, 2020, from https://www.history.com/topics/roaring-twenties/tulsa-race-massacre

[lxiii] History.com Editors. (2018, March 08). Tulsa Race Massacre. Retrieved May 31, 2020, from https://www.history.com/topics/roaring-twenties/tulsa-race-massacre

[lxiv] Hannon, K. (2018, September 09). Black Women Entrepreneurs: The Good And Not-So-Good News. Retrieved May 31, 2020, from https://www.forbes.com/sites/nextavenue/2018/09/09/black-women-entrepreneurs-the-good-and-not-so-good-news/

[lxv] NAACP. (2020). Criminal Justice Fact Sheet. Retrieved June 02, 2020, from https://www.naacp.org/criminal-justice-fact-sheet/

[lxvi] Ghandnoosh, N. (2019, June 06). Incarcerated Women and Girls. Retrieved June 02, 2020, from

https://www.sentencingproject.org/publications/incarcer ated-women-and-girls/

[lxvii] Thurgood Marshall Institute, L. (2019, March 15). Kemba Smith- The Thurgood Marshall Institute. Retrieved June 02, 2020, from https://tminstituteldf.org/kemba-smith/

[lxviii] Open Society (2006) Testimony of Kembra Smith https://opensocietypolicycenter.org/wp-content/uploads/Testimony-of-Kemba-Smith-vc.pdf

[lxix] Thurgood Marshall Institute, L. (2019, March 15). Kemba Smith- The Thurgood Marshall Institute. Retrieved June 02, 2020, from https://tminstituteldf.org/kemba-smith/

[lxx][lxx] *Leary, Joy DeGruy. (2005). Post traumatic slave syndrome : America's legacy of enduring injury and healing. Milwaukie, Oregon :Uptone Press*

[lxxi][lxxi] *Leary, Joy DeGruy. (2005). Post traumatic slave syndrome : America's legacy of enduring injury and healing. Milwaukie, Oregon :Uptone Press,*

[lxxii] *Leary, Joy DeGruy. (2005). Post traumatic slave syndrome : America's legacy of enduring injury and healing. Milwaukie, Oregon :Uptone Press,*

[lxxiii] Equal Pay Day. (2020). Equal Pay Day 2020. Retrieved June 02, 2020, from http://www.equalpaytoday.org/black-womens-equal-pay-day-2020

[lxxiv] Lui, M. (2006). *The color of wealth: The story behind the U.S. racial wealth divide.* New York: New Press. (33)

[lxxv] Lui, M. (2006). *The color of wealth: The story behind the U.S. racial wealth divide.* New York: New Press.

[lxxvi] Lui, M. (2006). *The color of wealth: The story behind the U.S. racial wealth divide.* New York: New Press.

[lxxvii] Lui, M. (2006). *The color of wealth: The story behind the U.S. racial wealth divide.* New York: New Press.

[lxxviii] Lui, M. (2006). *The color of wealth: The story behind the U.S. racial wealth divide.* New York: New Press.

[lxxix] History.com Editors. (2009, November 09). Trail of Tears. Retrieved June 02, 2020, from https://www.history.com/topics/native-american-history/trail-of-tears

[lxxx][lxxx] History.com Editors. (2009, November 09). Trail of Tears. Retrieved June 02, 2020, from

https://www.history.com/topics/native-american-history/trail-of-tears

[lxxxi] [lxxxi] Lui, M. (2006). *The color of wealth: The story behind the U.S. racial wealth divide*. New York: New Press.

[lxxxiii] Indian Country Today. (2003, September 08). Adamson: Land rich and dirt poor, the story of Native assets. Retrieved June 02, 2020, from https://indiancountrytoday.com/archive/adamson-land-rich-and-dirt-poor-the-story-of-native-assets-4iicEau730CJBPw6GF9beQ

[lxxxiv] Lui, M. (2006). *The color of wealth: The story behind the U.S. racial wealth divide*. New York: New Press.

[lxxxv] Chow, K. (2018, February 09). So What Exactly Is 'Blood Quantum'? Retrieved June 02, 2020, from https://www.npr.org/sections/codeswitch/2018/02/09/583987261/so-what-exactly-is-blood-quantum

[lxxxvi] Chow, K. (2018, February 09). So What Exactly Is 'Blood Quantum'? Retrieved June 02, 2020, from https://www.npr.org/sections/codeswitch/2018/02/09/583987261/so-what-exactly-is-blood-quantum

[lxxxvii][lxxxvii] Chow, K. (2018, February 09). So What Exactly Is 'Blood Quantum'? Retrieved June 02, 2020, from https://www.npr.org/sections/codeswitch/2018/02/09/583987261/so-what-exactly-is-blood-quantum

[lxxxviii] Lui, M. (2006). *The color of wealth: The story behind the U.S. racial wealth divide.* New York: New Press. (33)

[lxxxix] AAUW. (2020, March 31). The Simple Truth about the Pay Gap. Retrieved June 02, 2020, from https://www.aauw.org/resources/research/simple-truth/

[xc] Salam, M. (2019, April 12). Native American Women Are Facing a Crisis. Retrieved June 03, 2020, from https://www.nytimes.com/2019/04/12/us/native-american-women-violence.html

[xci] Salam, M. (2019, April 12). Native American Women Are Facing a Crisis. Retrieved June 03, 2020, from https://www.nytimes.com/2019/04/12/us/native-american-women-violence.html

[xcii] Salam, M. (2019, April 12). Native American Women Are Facing a Crisis. Retrieved June 03, 2020, from https://www.nytimes.com/2019/04/12/us/native-american-women-violence.html

[xciii] Salam, M. (2019, April 12). Native American Women Are Facing a Crisis. Retrieved June 03, 2020, from https://www.nytimes.com/2019/04/12/us/native-american-women-violence.html

[xciv] Bleir, G., & Zoledziowski, A. (2017). Murdered and missing Native American women challenge police and courts. Retrieved June 03, 2020, from https://publicintegrity.org/politics/murdered-and-missing-native-american-women-challenge-police-and-courts/

[xcvi] Hummel, B. (2016, July 12). Historical Trauma: The Confluence of Mental Health and History in Native American Communities. Retrieved June 03, 2020, from https://medium.com/@bradyhummel/historical-trauma-the-confluence-of-mental-health-and-history-in-native-american-communities-5513985836c5

Hummel, B. (2016, July 12). Historical Trauma: The Confluence of Mental Health and History in Native American Communities. Retrieved June 03, 2020, from https://medium.com/@bradyhummel/historical-trauma-the-confluence-of-mental-health-and-history-in-native-american-communities-5513985836c5

[xcvii] Balsamo, M., & Fonseca, F. (2019, November 22). Attorney general unveils plan to help missing Native American women. Retrieved June 03, 2020, from https://www.pbs.org/newshour/nation/attorney-general-unveils-plan-to-help-missing-native-american-women

[xcviii] Wagner, A. (2017, March 06). America's Forgotten History of Illegal Deportations. Retrieved June 03, 2020, from https://www.theatlantic.com/politics/archive/2017/03/americas-brutal-forgotten-history-of-illegal-deportations/517971/

[xcix] Balderrama, F. E., & Rodriguez, R. (1995). **Decade of betrayal: Mexican repatriation in the 1930s.** Albuquerque: University of New **Mexico** Press.

[c] Bender (2003)Greasers and Gringos: Latinos, Law, and the American Imagination (Critical America)

[ci] Funderburk, B. (2017, September 04). Operation Wetback. Retrieved June 03, 2020, from https://www.britannica.com/topic/Operation-Wetback

[cii] Blakemore, E. (2018, March 23). The Largest Mass Deportation in American History. Retrieved June 03, 2020, from https://www.history.com/news/operation-wetback-eisenhower-1954-deportation

[ciii] Gándara, P. (2015). *Fulfilling Americas Future* [Pamphlet]. Washington, DC: The White House Initiative on Educational Excellence for Hispanics.

[civ] Gándara, P. (2015). *Fulfilling Americas Future* [Pamphlet]. Washington, DC: The White House Initiative on Educational Excellence for Hispanics.

[cv] Allen, K. (2016, September 23). Gender pay gap won't close until 2069, says Deloitte. Retrieved June 03, 2020, from https://www.theguardian.com/society/2016/sep/24/gender-pay-gap-wont-close-until-2069-says-deloitte

[cvi] Prosperity Now (2019) https://prosperitynow.org/blog/racial-wealth-snapshot-latino-americans

[cvii] Leiva, L. (n.d.). 10 Latinas Share What They Wish They'd Known At The Start Of Their Careers. Retrieved June 03, 2020, from https://www.refinery29.com/en-us/latina-equal-pay-day-2018

[cviii] U.S. Department of Health and Human Service (2017) Youth Risk Behavior Surveillance — United States, 2017 https://www.cdc.gov/healthyyouth/data/yrbs/pdf/2017/ss6708.pdf

[cix] Passel, J., & Cohn, D. (2020, May 30). U.S. Population Projections: 2005-2050. Retrieved June 03, 2020, from https://www.pewresearch.org/hispanic/2008/02/11/us-population-projections-2005-2050/

[cx] SAMHSA - Substance Abuse and Mental Health Services ... (n.d.). Retrieved June 3, 2020, from https://www.samhsa.gov/

[cxi] Roddick, M. (2016, September 14). The 8 Dimensions of Wellness: Where Do You Fit In? Retrieved June 03, 2020, from https://www.goodtherapy.org/blog/8-dimensions-of-wellness-where-do-you-fit-in-0527164

[cxii] Khazan, O. (2014, May 19). Thomas Edison and the Cult of Sleep Deprivation. Retrieved June 03, 2020, from https://www.theatlantic.com/health/archive/2014/05/thomas-edison-and-the-cult-of-sleep-deprivation/370824/

[cxiii] Khazan, O. (2014, May 19). Thomas Edison and the Cult of Sleep Deprivation. Retrieved June 03, 2020, from https://www.theatlantic.com/health/archive/2014/05/thomas-edison-and-the-cult-of-sleep-deprivation/370824/

[cxiv] How Sleep Deprivation Costs the Economy and our Public Health. (2019, July 19). Retrieved June 03, 2020, from https://www.tuck.com/economics-of-sleep/

[cxv] How Sleep Deprivation Costs the Economy and our Public Health. (2019, July 19). Retrieved June 03, 2020, from https://www.tuck.com/economics-of-sleep/

[cxvi] Hafner, M., Stepanek, M., Taylor, J., Troxel, W., & Van Stolk, C. (2017, January 1). Why Sleep Matters-The Economic Costs of Insufficient Sleep: A Cross-Country Comparative Analysis. Retrieved June 03, 2020, from https://www.ncbi.nlm.nih.gov/pmc/articles/PMC5627640/

[cxvii] Hafner, M., Stepanek, M., Taylor, J., Troxel, W., & Van Stolk, C. (2017, January 1). Why Sleep Matters-The Economic Costs of Insufficient Sleep: A Cross-Country Comparative Analysis. Retrieved June 03, 2020, from https://www.ncbi.nlm.nih.gov/pmc/articles/PMC5627640/

[cxviii] Hafner, M., Stepanek, M., Taylor, J., Troxel, W., & Van Stolk, C. (2017, January 1). Why Sleep Matters-The Economic Costs of Insufficient Sleep: A Cross-Country Comparative Analysis. Retrieved June 03, 2020, from https://www.ncbi.nlm.nih.gov/pmc/articles/PMC5627640/

[cxix] Garone, S. (2020, February 24). Mood Journal 101: How to Get Started on Controlling Your Emotions. Retrieved June 03, 2020, from https://www.healthline.com/health/how-to-keep-mood-journal

[cxx] Take the ACE Quiz – And Learn What It Does and Doesn't Mean. (2019, May 30). Retrieved June 03, 2020, from https://developingchild.harvard.edu/media-

coverage/take-the-ace-quiz-and-learn-what-it-does-and-doesnt-mean/

[cxxi] Seven Dimensions of Wellness. (n.d.). Retrieved June 03, 2020, from https://www.grcc.edu/humanresources/wellness/sevendi mensionsofwellness

[cxxii] Miller, C. (2015, December 24). The typical American lives only 18 miles from Mom - The Boston Globe. Retrieved June 03, 2020, from https://www.bostonglobe.com/news/nation/2015/12/24/t he-typical-american-lives-only-miles-from-mom/iSYQglkxaqA0VUe3WWHt7K/story.html

[cxxiii] Miller, C. (2015, December 24). The typical American lives only 18 miles from Mom - The Boston Globe. Retrieved June 03, 2020, from https://www.bostonglobe.com/news/nation/2015/12/24/t he-typical-american-lives-only-miles-from-mom/iSYQglkxaqA0VUe3WWHt7K/story.html

[cxxiv][cxxiv] Geary, A. (2016, November 22). Eight simple steps to increase your intellectual wellness - News - Illinois State. Retrieved June 03, 2020, from https://news.illinoisstate.edu/2014/03/seven-simple-steps-increase-intellectual-wellness/

[cxxv] Allen, S. (n.d.). Eight Reasons Why Awe Makes Your Life Better. Retrieved June 03, 2020, from

https://greatergood.berkeley.edu/article/item/eight_reas
ons_why_awe_makes_your_life_better

[cxxvi] Allen, S. (n.d.). Eight Reasons Why Awe Makes Your Life Better. Retrieved June 03, 2020, from https://greatergood.berkeley.edu/article/item/eight_reas ons_why_awe_makes_your_life_better

[cxxvii] Allen, S. (n.d.). Eight Reasons Why Awe Makes Your Life Better. Retrieved June 03, 2020, from https://greatergood.berkeley.edu/article/item/eight_reas ons_why_awe_makes_your_life_better

[cxxviii] Masci, D. (2018, February 07). 5 facts about blacks and religion in America. Retrieved June 03, 2020, from https://www.pewresearch.org/fact-tank/2018/02/07/5-facts-about-the-religious-lives-of-african-americans/

[cxxix] CONSUMER EXPENDITURES--2018. (2019, September 10). Retrieved June 03, 2020, from https://www.bls.gov/news.release/cesan.nr0.htm

[cxxx] Admin, M. (n.d.). Home. Retrieved June 03, 2020, from https://www.financialtherapyassociation.org/

[cxxxii] Konsko, L. (2020, May 05). How Young Is Too Young to Start Building Credit? Retrieved June 03, 2020, from https://www.nerdwallet.com/blog/finance/how-young-start-building-credit/

[cxxxiii] 12-Step Programs & Meetings: How They Work. (n.d.). Retrieved June 03, 2020, from https://deserthopetreatment.com/alcohol-abuse/12-step-program/

[cxxxiv] Josephson, A. (2019, December 12). The Difference Between a Financial Counselor and a Financial Planner. Retrieved June 03, 2020, from https://smartasset.com/retirement/the-difference-between-a-financial-counselor-and-a-financial-planner

[cxxxv] Archelta, K (n.d) Financial Therapy Association Counseling https://www.kitces.com/blog/kristy-archuleta-kansas-state-university-of-georgia-podcast-financial-therapy-association-counseling-communication/

[cxxxvi]

[cxxxvii]FINRA (n.d) professional requirements https://www.finra.org/#/

[cxxxviii] Registered Financial Professionals. (n.d.). Retrieved June 03, 2020, from https://www.finra.org/investors/learn-to-invest/choosing-investment-professional/registered-financial-professionals

[cxxxix] Accounting Job Description: What You'll Do. (2019, September 13). Retrieved June 03, 2020, from

https://www.allbusinessschools.com/accounting/job-description/

[cxl] Certified Public Accountant (CPA). (n.d.). Retrieved June 03, 2020, from https://www.aicpa-cima.com/designations-certifications/certified-public-accountant-cpa.html

[cxli] CFP Board. (n.d.). Retrieved June 03, 2020, from http://www.cfp.net/

Endnotes

_____

_____

_____

_____

_____

_____

_____

_____

_____

_____

_____

_____

_____

_____

_____

_____

ENDNOTES

_____

_____

_____

_____

_____

_____

_____

_____

_____

_____

_____

_____

_____

_____

_____

_____

_____

_____

_____

Endnotes

_____

_____

_____

_____

_____

_____

_____

_____

_____

_____

_____

_____

_____

_____

_____

_____

CPSIA information can be obtained
at www.ICGtesting.com
Printed in the USA
LVHW021514170720
660993LV00010B/362

9 781734 600209